CANADA

THE WEST
pages 98–121

THE
MIDWEST
pages 62–87

THE
NORTHEAST
pages 12–35

ATLANTIC
OCEAN

THE
SOUTHWEST
pages 88–97

THE SOUTHEAST
pages 36–61

GULF OF
MEXICO

MEXICO

BAHAMAS

CUBA

NATIONAL GEOGRAPHIC KIDS™

BEGINNER'S UNITED STATES ATLAS

It's YOUR country. Be a part of it!

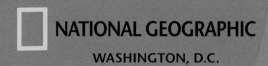

NATIONAL GEOGRAPHIC

WASHINGTON, D.C.

Table of Contents

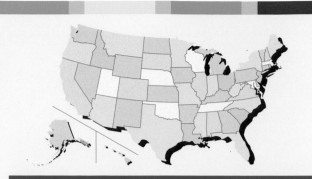

What is a Map?

An atlas is a collection of maps and pictures. A map is a drawing of a place as it looks from above. It is flat, and it is smaller than the place it shows. Learning to read a map can help you find where you are and where you want to go. **Mapping your home...**

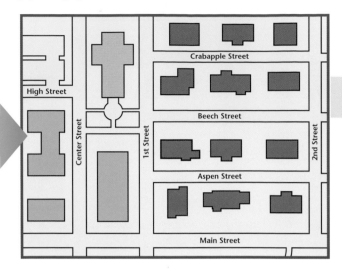

From a bird's-eye view...

if you were a bird flying directly overhead, you would see only the tops of things. You wouldn't see walls, tree trunks, tires, or feet.

On a large-scale map...

you see places from a bird's-eye view. But a map uses drawings called symbols to show things on the ground, such as houses or streets. The map of Washington, D.C., on page 10 is an example of a large-scale map.

Finding places on the map

A **map** can help you get where you want to go. A map helps you read it by showing you north, south, east and west, a key, and a scale.

▶ A **compass rose** helps you travel in the right direction. It tells you where north (N), south (S), east (E), and west (W) are on your map. Often only a north arrow is used.

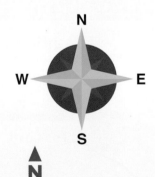

▶ A **map key** helps you understand the symbols used by the mapmaker to show things like buildings, towns, or rivers on the map.

- ✪ Country capital
- ★ State capital
- ● ● City or town
- ⋯⋯ Boundary
- ▧ Indian Reservation
- ▧ State Park
- ▧ National Park
- ▧ National Forest
- ▧ National Grassland
- ▧ National Wildlife Refuge

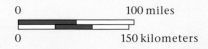

◀ A **scale** tells you about distance on a map. The scale shows what length on the map represents the labeled distance on the ground.

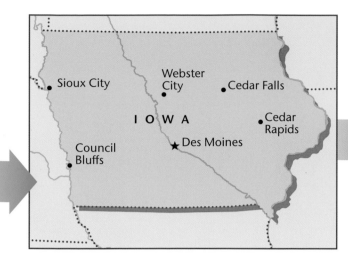

On an intermediate-scale map...

you see a place from much higher up.
A town appears as a tiny dot. You can't see
houses, but you can see more of the land
around the town. Most maps in this
atlas show a whole state with its towns
and other special features.

On a small-scale map...

you can see much more of the country around
the state, including other states. But on a small-
scale map there is much less detail. You can
no longer see most features within the state.
Two states—Alaska and Hawai'i—are often
shown in separate boxes or on a map of the
whole continent, like on pages 6 and 7.

Map Key for the State Maps

- •Aspen ....*town of under 25,000 residents*
- •Frankfort ....*town of 25,000 to 99,999*
- •San Jose ....*city of 100,000 to 999,999*
- •New York ....*city of 1,000,000 and over*
- ⊛ National capital
- ★ State capital
- ▪ Point of interest
- + Mountain peak with elevation above sea level
- • Low point with elevation below sea level
- —— River
- – – – Intermittent river
- ⊥⊥⊥⊥ Canal
- —— Interstate or selected other highway
- - - - - - Trail
- ·········· State or national boundary
- ·········· Continental divide
- ⬭ Lake
- ⬭ Intermittent lake

- ∷∷∷ Dry Lake
- Swamp
- Glacier
- Sand
- Lava
- Area below sea level
- Indian Reservation, **I.R.**
- State Park, **S.P.**
- National Historic Park, **N.H.P.**
  National Lakeshore
  National Monument, **NAT. MON.**
  National Park, **N.P.**
  National Preserve, **N. PRES.**
  National Recreation Area, **N.R.A.**
  National River
  National Scenic Area
  National Seashore
  National Volcanic Monument
- National Forest, **N.F.**
- National Grassland, **N.G.**
- National Wildlife Refuge, **N.W.R.**

The Physical United States

The Land

 Land regions The rugged Sierra Nevadas and Rocky Mountains run north to south through the western United States. Between these mountains are dry lands with little vegetation. East of the Rockies are wide grassy plains and the older, lower Appalachian Mountains.

 Water The Mississippi–Missouri is the longest river system in the United States. The Great Lakes are the largest freshwater lakes in the country.

 Climate The United States has many climate types—from cold Alaska to tropical Hawai'i, with milder climates in the other 48 states.

 Plants The United States has forests where there is plenty of rain. Grasslands cover drier areas.

 Animals There are many kinds of animals—everything from bears and deer to songbirds large and small.

◀ North America is famous for its **deciduous forests**. Leaves turn fiery colors each fall!

▲ Waves off the Pacific Ocean roll onto a beach along the shore of Molokai, one of the islands that make up the state of Hawai'i.

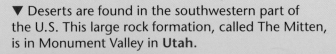

▼ Deserts are found in the southwestern part of the U.S. This large rock formation, called The Mitten, is in Monument Valley in **Utah.**

◀ The majestic bald eagle is the national bird of the United States. It is found throughout the country, but about half live in **Alaska.**

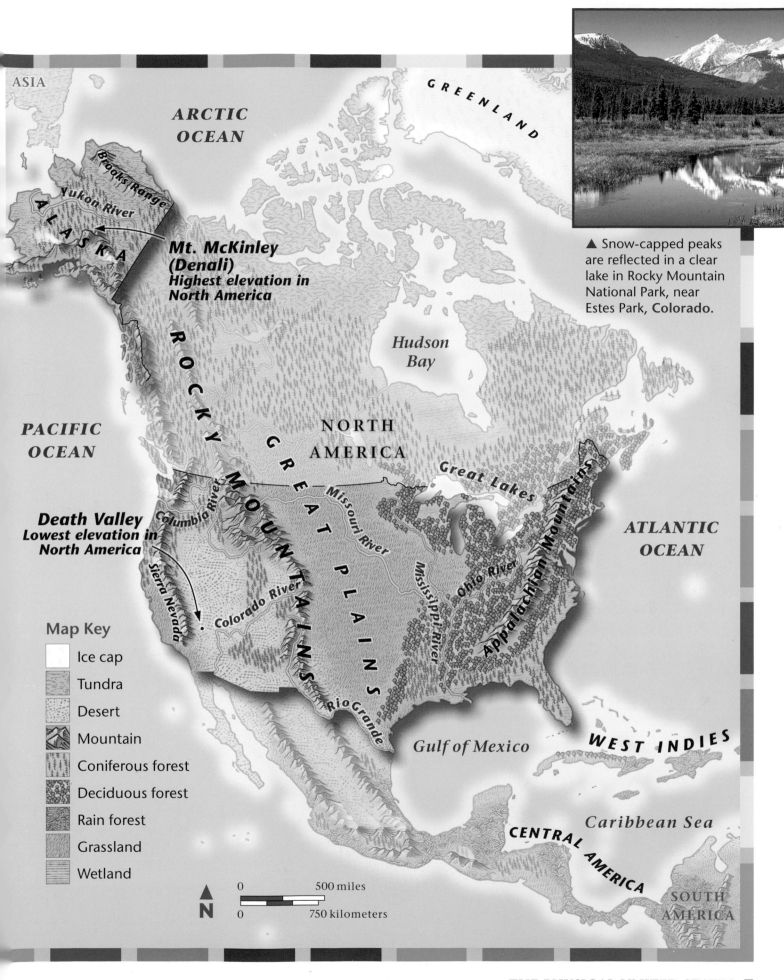

ASIA

ARCTIC OCEAN

GREENLAND

Brooks Range

Yukon River

ALASKA

Mt. McKinley (Denali)
Highest elevation in North America

PACIFIC OCEAN

ROCKY MOUNTAINS

Hudson Bay

NORTH AMERICA

Death Valley
Lowest elevation in North America

Sierra Nevada

Columbia River

GREAT PLAINS

Missouri River

Great Lakes

Mississippi River

Ohio River

Appalachian Mountains

ATLANTIC OCEAN

Colorado River

Rio Grande

Gulf of Mexico

WEST INDIES

Caribbean Sea

CENTRAL AMERICA

SOUTH AMERICA

▲ Snow-capped peaks are reflected in a clear lake in Rocky Mountain National Park, near Estes Park, **Colorado**.

Map Key

- Ice cap
- Tundra
- Desert
- Mountain
- Coniferous forest
- Deciduous forest
- Rain forest
- Grassland
- Wetland

N

0   500 miles

0   750 kilometers

The Political United States

The People

![flags icon] **States** The United States is made up of 50 states. Alaska and Hawai'i are separated from the rest of the country. So you can see them close up, they are shown near the bottom of the map.

![city icon] **Cities** Washington, D.C., is the national capital. Each state also has a capital city. New York City has the most people.

![person icon] **People** The United States is made up of people from almost every country in the world. Most live and work in and around cities.

![languages icon] **Languages** English is the main language, followed by Spanish.

![products icon] **Products** The main products include cars, machinery, petroleum, natural gas, coal, beef, wheat, and forest products.

▲ Chinese New Year is a big celebration in **San Francisco**. Many Chinese-Americans live there.

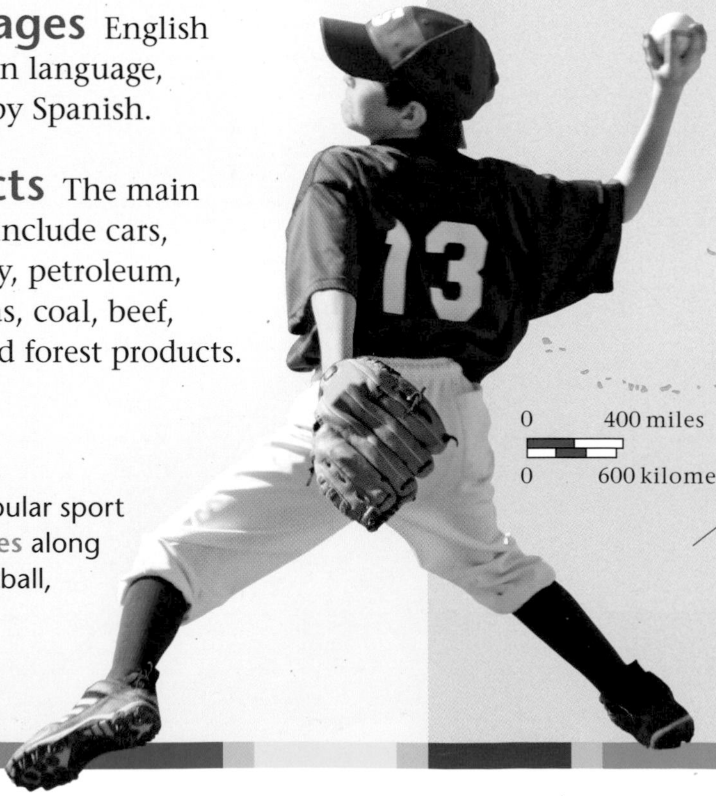

▶ Baseball is a popular sport in the **United States** along with soccer, basketball, and football.

Seattle •
Olympia ★
WASHINGTON
Portland •
★ Salem
OREGON
Columbia River
IDAHO
★ Boise
C A L I F O R N I A
Sacramento ★
Carson City ★
Salt Lake City ★
NEVADA
UT
• San Francisco
San Jose •
• Las Vegas
Los Angeles •
ARIZO
San Diego •
Phoenix ★
Tucson •

PACIFIC OCEAN

ALASKA
Juneau ★

0   400 miles
0   600 kilometers

HAWAI'I
Honolulu ★

0   150 miles
0   200 kilometers

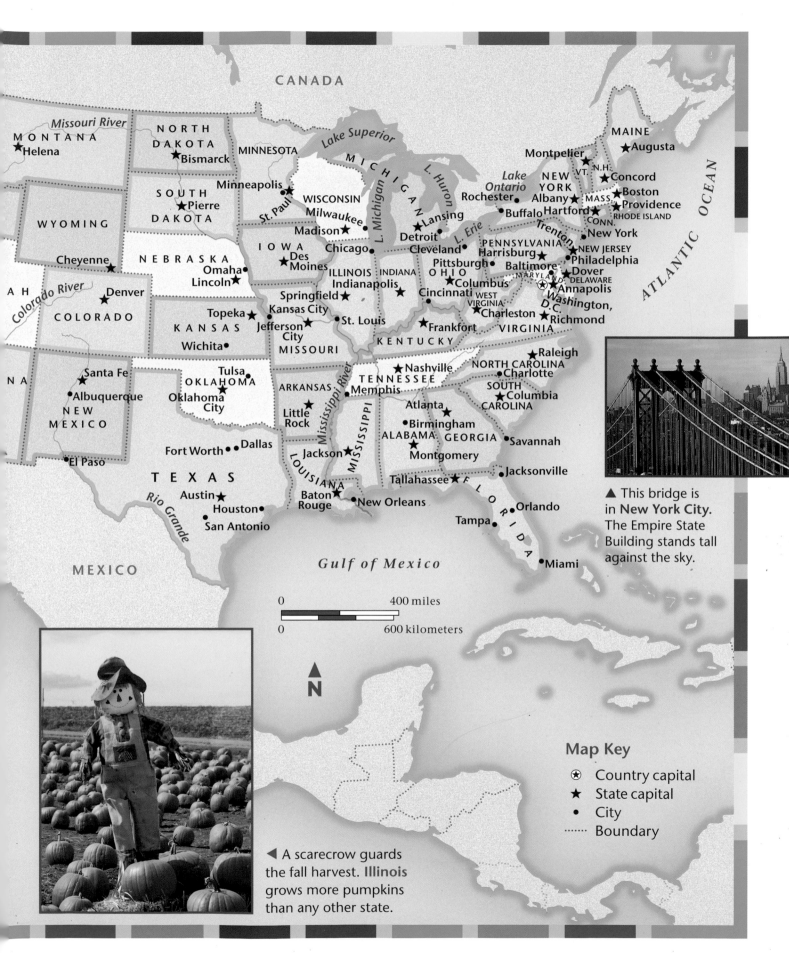

CANADA

Missouri River

MONTANA
★ Helena

NORTH DAKOTA
★ Bismarck

MINNESOTA

Lake Superior

MICHIGAN

L. Huron

MAINE
★ Augusta

Montpelier

Minneapolis
★ St. Paul

SOUTH DAKOTA
★ Pierre

WISCONSIN
• Milwaukee
★ Madison

L. Michigan

★ Lansing

Detroit

Lake Ontario

NEW YORK

Rochester

Albany

VT.
N.H.
★ Concord

MASS.
★ Boston
★ Providence

WYOMING

★ Cheyenne

IOWA
★ Des Moines

Chicago

Cleveland

L. Erie

Buffalo

Hartford

CONN.
RHODE ISLAND

Trenton

NEBRASKA
• Omaha
★ Lincoln

ILLINOIS

INDIANA

OHIO

PENNSYLVANIA
Harrisburg ★

Pittsburgh

New York

NEW JERSEY
★ Philadelphia

Colorado River

A H

★ Denver

COLORADO

★ Indianapolis

Springfield ★

Columbus ★

Cincinnati

Baltimore

Dover

MARYLAND
⊛ Annapolis

DELAWARE

Washington, D.C.

N A

★ Topeka

Kansas City

★ Jefferson City

Wichita •

KANSAS

St. Louis •

MISSOURI

WEST VIRGINIA
★ Charleston

Richmond ★

VIRGINIA

Santa Fe ★

OKLAHOMA
★ Tulsa

KENTUCKY
★ Frankfort

Raleigh ★

N A

• Albuquerque

NEW MEXICO

Oklahoma City ★

ARKANSAS

TENNESSEE
★ Nashville

Memphis ★

NORTH CAROLINA
★ Charlotte

SOUTH CAROLINA
★ Columbia

Little Rock ★

• El Paso

Fort Worth • • Dallas

Jackson ★

MISSISSIPPI

Atlanta ★

• Birmingham

ALABAMA

GEORGIA

• Savannah

TEXAS

Rio Grande

Austin ★

• Houston

San Antonio •

LOUISIANA

Baton Rouge ★

Montgomery ★

Tallahassee ★

FLORIDA

Jacksonville •

• New Orleans

Orlando •

MEXICO

Gulf of Mexico

Tampa •

• Miami

ATLANTIC OCEAN

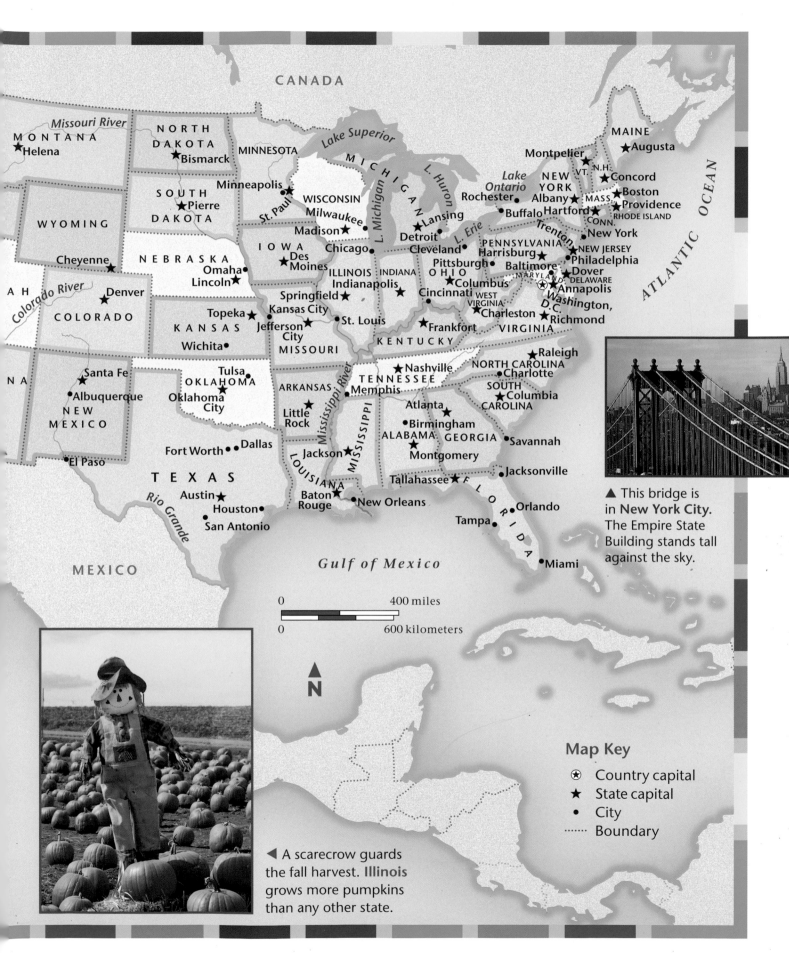

▲ This bridge is in **New York City.** The Empire State Building stands tall against the sky.

0 ————— 400 miles

0 ————— 600 kilometers

N

◀ A scarecrow guards the fall harvest. **Illinois** grows more pumpkins than any other state.

Map Key

⊛ Country capital

★ State capital

• City

····· Boundary

THE POLITICAL UNITED STATES **9**

The District of Columbia

The National Capital Washington, D.C.

 Land & Water The National Mall, the Potomac River, and the Anacostia River are important land and water features of the District of Columbia.

Statehood The District of Columbia was founded in 1790, but it is not a state.

People & Places The District of Columbia's population is 591,833. Known as Washington, D.C., the city is the seat of the U.S. government.

Fun Fact The flag of the District of Columbia, with three red stars and two red stripes, is based on the shield in George Washington's family coat of arms.

▶ The **Smithsonian Institution**, the world's largest museum, is actually made up of 19 museums. It was established in 1846 and is some-times referred to as the nation's attic because of its large collections.

◀ **Abraham Lincoln**, who was President during the Civil War and a strong opponent of slavery, is remembered in a memorial that houses this seated statue at the west end of the National Mall.

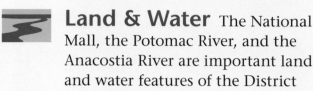

Washington, D.C., Flag

American Beauty Rose

Wood Thrush

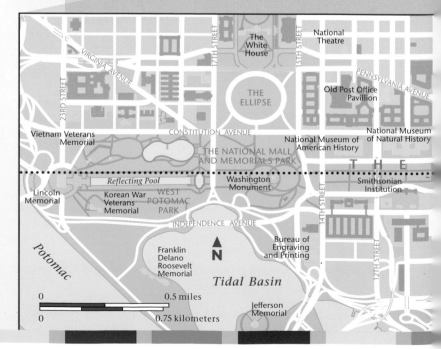

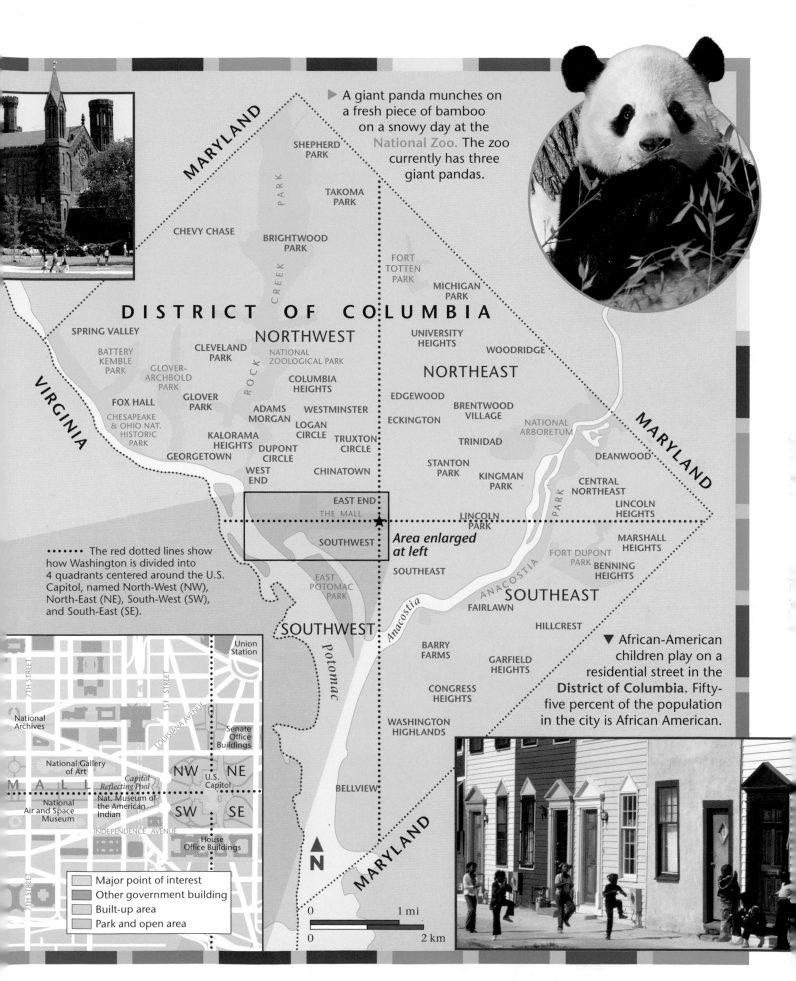

A giant panda munches on a fresh piece of bamboo on a snowy day at the **National Zoo.** The zoo currently has three giant pandas.

MARYLAND

SHEPHERD PARK

TAKOMA PARK

CHEVY CHASE

BRIGHTWOOD PARK

PARK

CREEK

FORT TOTTEN PARK

MICHIGAN PARK

DISTRICT OF COLUMBIA

SPRING VALLEY

NORTHWEST

UNIVERSITY HEIGHTS

WOODRIDGE

BATTERY KEMBLE PARK

CLEVELAND PARK

NATIONAL ZOOLOGICAL PARK

ROCK

NORTHEAST

GLOVER-ARCHBOLD PARK

COLUMBIA HEIGHTS

EDGEWOOD

FOX HALL

GLOVER PARK

ADAMS MORGAN

WESTMINSTER

ECKINGTON

BRENTWOOD VILLAGE

NATIONAL ARBORETUM

CHESAPEAKE & OHIO NAT. HISTORIC PARK

LOGAN CIRCLE

TRINIDAD

VIRGINIA

KALORAMA HEIGHTS

GEORGETOWN

DUPONT CIRCLE

TRUXTON CIRCLE

STANTON PARK

KINGMAN PARK

DEANWOOD

WEST END

CHINATOWN

PARK

CENTRAL NORTHEAST

EAST END

LINCOLN HEIGHTS

THE MALL

LINCOLN PARK

Area enlarged at left

MARSHALL HEIGHTS

SOUTHWEST

FORT DUPONT PARK

BENNING HEIGHTS

•••••• The red dotted lines show how Washington is divided into 4 quadrants centered around the U.S. Capitol, named North-West (NW), North-East (NE), South-West (SW), and South-East (SE).

EAST POTOMAC PARK

SOUTHEAST

ANACOSTIA

SOUTHEAST

FAIRLAWN

HILLCREST

SOUTHWEST

Anacostia

potomac

BARRY FARMS

GARFIELD HEIGHTS

▼ African-American children play on a residential street in the **District of Columbia.** Fifty-five percent of the population in the city is African American.

CONGRESS HEIGHTS

WASHINGTON HIGHLANDS

BELLVIEW

7TH STREET

Union Station

1ST STREET

LOUISIANA AVENUE

National Archives

Senate Office Buildings

National Gallery of Art

M A L L

Capitol Reflecting Pool

NW U.S. Capitol

NE

National Air and Space Museum

Nat. Museum of the American Indian

SW SE

INDEPENDENCE AVENUE

House Office Buildings

7TH STREET

MARYLAND

▲ N

0   1 mi

0   2 km

Major point of interest
Other government building
Built-up area
Park and open area

The Northeast

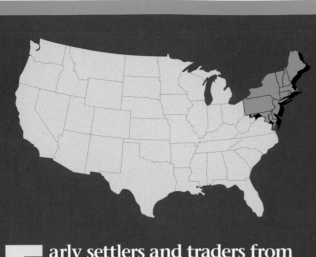

Early settlers and traders from Europe established colonies in the Northeast region. These colonies eventually became states. Over time, people came from countries all around the world to live in the United States. Many of these people arrived through large port cities in the Northeast, including New York City, Boston, and Baltimore. They brought with them different customs, languages, and beliefs that make the Northeast a region of great variety. Today the Northeast region includes the country's financial center, New York City, and its political capital, Washington, D.C.

Water plunges as much as 110 feet (34 m) over the American Falls on the Niagara River near New York's border with Canada, our neighbor to the north. Black bears are common in the forests of the region.

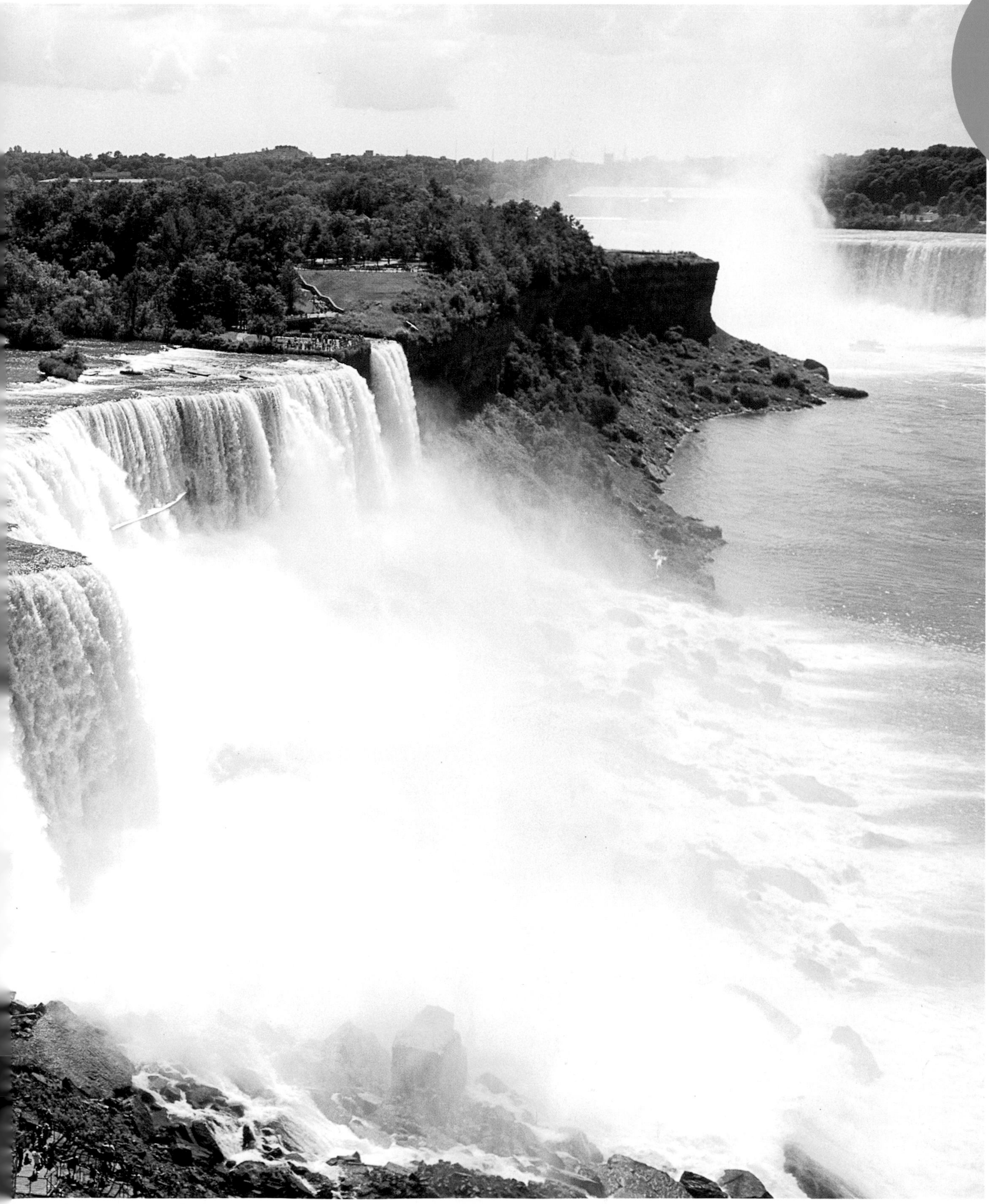

The Northeast

Connecticut

Land & Water Mount Frissell, the Connecticut River, and Long Island Sound are important land and water features of Connecticut.

Statehood Connecticut became the 5th state in 1788.

People & Places Connecticut's population is 3,501,252. Hartford is the state capital. The largest city is Bridgeport.

Fun Fact The sperm whale, Connecticut's state animal, is known for its massive head. Its brain is larger than that of any other creature known to have lived on Earth.

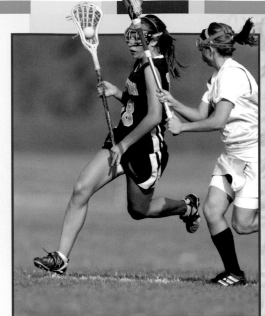

▲ Girls' lacrosse is popular in schools and colleges in **Connecticut** and across the U.S. It was adapted from a Native American game.

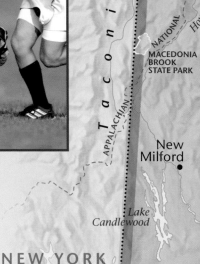

Connecticut State Flag

Mountain Laurel State Flower

Robin State Bird

◀ The *Charles W. Morgan*, launched in 1841, but now docked in **Mystic Seaport**, is the last surviving wooden whaling ship in the U.S.

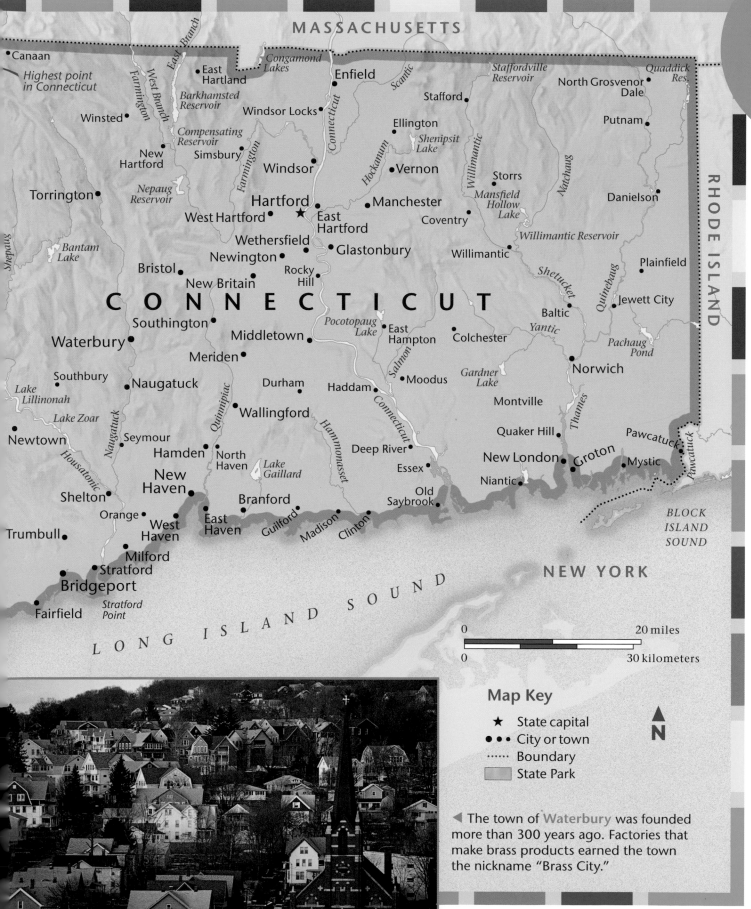

MASSACHUSETTS

RHODE ISLAND

Canaan

*Highest point
in Connecticut*

East Branch

West Branch Farmington

East
Hartland

*Congamond
Lakes*

Enfield

Scantic

*Staffordville
Reservoir*

North Grosvenor
Dale

*Quaddick
Res.*

*Barkhamsted
Reservoir*

Stafford

Winsted

Windsor Locks

Ellington

*Shenipsit
Lake*

Putnam

*Compensating
Reservoir*

Simsbury

New
Hartford

Windsor

Vernon

Storrs

Danielson

Hockanum

Willimantic

Torrington

Farmington

*Nepaug
Reservoir*

Connecticut

*Mansfield
Hollow
Lake*

Hartford

Manchester

Natchaug

Shepaug

*Bantam
Lake*

West Hartford

East
Hartford

Coventry

Willimantic Reservoir

Wethersfield

Glastonbury

Willimantic

Plainfield

Bristol

Newington

Rocky
Hill

C O N N E C T I C U T

Shetucket

Quinebaug

New Britain

Jewett City

Southington

Middletown

*Pocotopaug
Lake*

East
Hampton

Colchester

Yantic

Baltic

*Pachaug
Pond*

Waterbury

Meriden

Salmon

Moodus

*Gardner
Lake*

Norwich

Southbury

Naugatuck

Durham

Haddam

Montville

*Lake
Lillinonah*

Quinnipiac

Connecticut

Quaker Hill

Thames

Pawcatuck

Pawcatuck

Lake Zoar

Wallingford

Hammonasset

Deep River

New London

Groton

Mystic

Newtown

Housatonic

Naugatuck

Seymour

Hamden

North
Haven

*Lake
Gaillard*

Essex

Niantic

*BLOCK
ISLAND
SOUND*

Shelton

New
Haven

Branford

Old
Saybrook

Orange

East
Haven

Guilford

Madison

Clinton

NEW YORK

Trumbull

West
Haven

Milford

Stratford

Bridgeport

*Stratford
Point*

Fairfield

L O N G   I S L A N D   S O U N D

| 0 | | | | 20 miles |
| 0 | | | | 30 kilometers |

Map Key

★ State capital
••• City or town
······ Boundary
▨ State Park

N

◀ The town of **Waterbury** was founded
more than 300 years ago. Factories that
make brass products earned the town
the nickname "Brass City."

Delaware

Land & Water Barrier Islands, Cypress Swamp, and Delaware Bay are important land and water features of Delaware.

Statehood Delaware became the 1st state in 1787.

People & Places Delaware's population is 873,092. Dover is the state capital. The largest city is Wilmington.

Fun Fact Each year contestants bring pumpkins and launching machines to the Punkin Chunkin World Championship in Bridgeville to see who can toss their big orange squash the farthest.

▲ The Delmarva Peninsula, with nearly 2,000 poultry growers, is a major producing area for chickens. The industry's trade association is located in **Georgetown**.

▶ Patriotic boys wave American flags at a Delaware Motorsports track near **Delmar**. Racing fans have come to the tracks since they opened in 1963.

▼ Bright-colored umbrellas dot **Bethany Beach**. Sun, sand, and surf attract thousands of vacationers each year to Delaware's shore.

DECEMBER 7. 1787

Delaware State Flag

Peach Blossom State Flower

Blue Hen Chicken State Bird

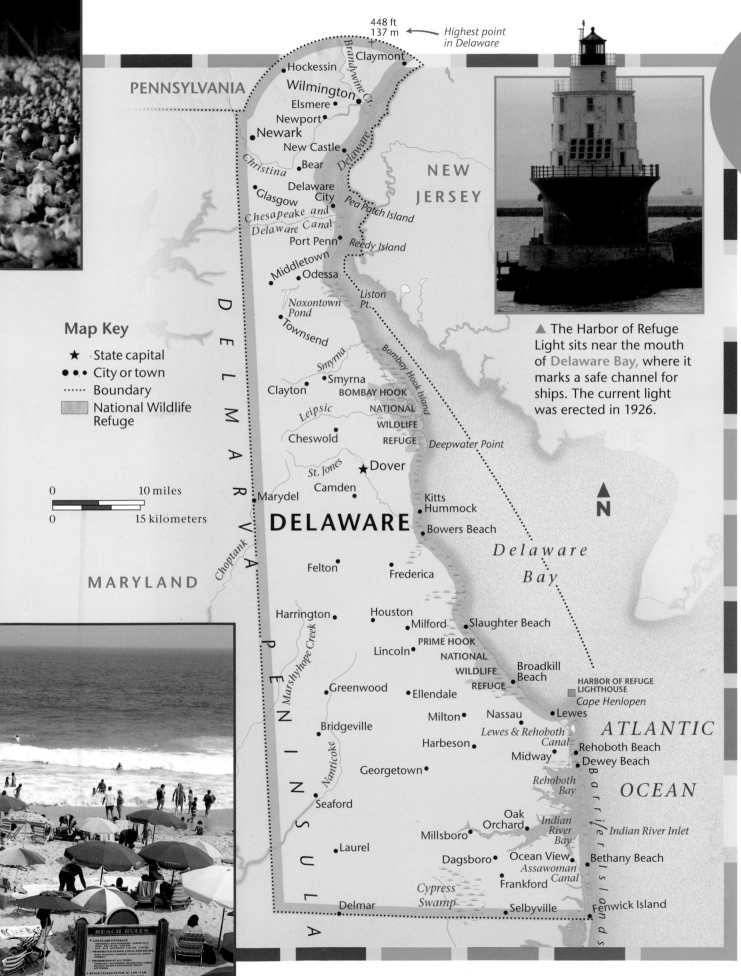

448 ft
137 m ← *Highest point in Delaware*

PENNSYLVANIA

Claymont
Hockessin
Wilmington
Elsmere
Newport
Newark
New Castle
Bear
Brandywine Cr.
Christina
Delaware

NEW JERSEY

Delaware City
Glasgow
Chesapeake and Delaware Canal
Pea Patch Island
Port Penn
Reedy Island
Middletown
Odessa
Liston Pt.
Noxontown Pond
Townsend
Bombay Hook Island
Smyrna
Smyrna
Clayton
BOMBAY HOOK NATIONAL WILDLIFE REFUGE
Leipsic
Cheswold
Deepwater Point

▲ The Harbor of Refuge Light sits near the mouth of Delaware Bay, where it marks a safe channel for ships. The current light was erected in 1926.

Map Key

★ State capital
••• City or town
..... Boundary
▨ National Wildlife Refuge

0 ———— 10 miles
0 ———— 15 kilometers

St. Jones
★ Dover
Camden
Marydel

DELAWARE

Kitts Hummock
Bowers Beach

Felton
Frederica

MARYLAND

Choptank

Delaware Bay

N

Harrington
Houston
Milford
Slaughter Beach
Lincoln
PRIME HOOK NATIONAL WILDLIFE REFUGE
Broadkill Beach
Greenwood
Ellendale
HARBOR OF REFUGE LIGHTHOUSE
Cape Henlopen
Milton
Nassau
Lewes
Bridgeville
Lewes & Rehoboth Canal
Harbeson
Midway
Rehoboth Beach
Dewey Beach

ATLANTIC

Marshyhope Creek

Georgetown
Rehoboth Bay

OCEAN

Seaford
Nanticoke

Oak Orchard
Indian River Bay
Indian River Inlet
Millsboro
Laurel
Dagsboro
Ocean View
Bethany Beach
Assawoman Canal
Frankford
Cypress Swamp
Delmar
Selbyville
Fenwick Island

DELMARVA PENINSULA

Barrier Islands

The Northeast

Maine

Land & Water The Appalachian Mountains, Mt. Katahdin, and the Gulf of Maine are important land and water features of Maine.

Statehood Maine became the 23rd state in 1820.

People & Places Maine's population is 1,316,456. Augusta is the state capital. The largest city is Portland.

Fun Fact During the last ice age, glaciers carved hundreds of bays and inlets along Maine's shoreline and created some 2,000 islands off the coast.

▲ More than 60 lighthouses line Maine's rocky coastline, warning ships of danger. The oldest lighthouse, Portland Head Light, is located at Cape Elizabeth.

◀ Each year **Rockland** hosts the Maine Lobster Festival. This celebration of the state's popular seafood delicacy attracts visitors from far and near.

▼ Moose are North America's largest deer, averaging 6 feet (2 m) tall at the shoulders. This female stands knee-deep in grass near **Rangeley Lake**.

Maine State Flag

White Pine Cone and Tassel State Flower

Chickadee State Bird

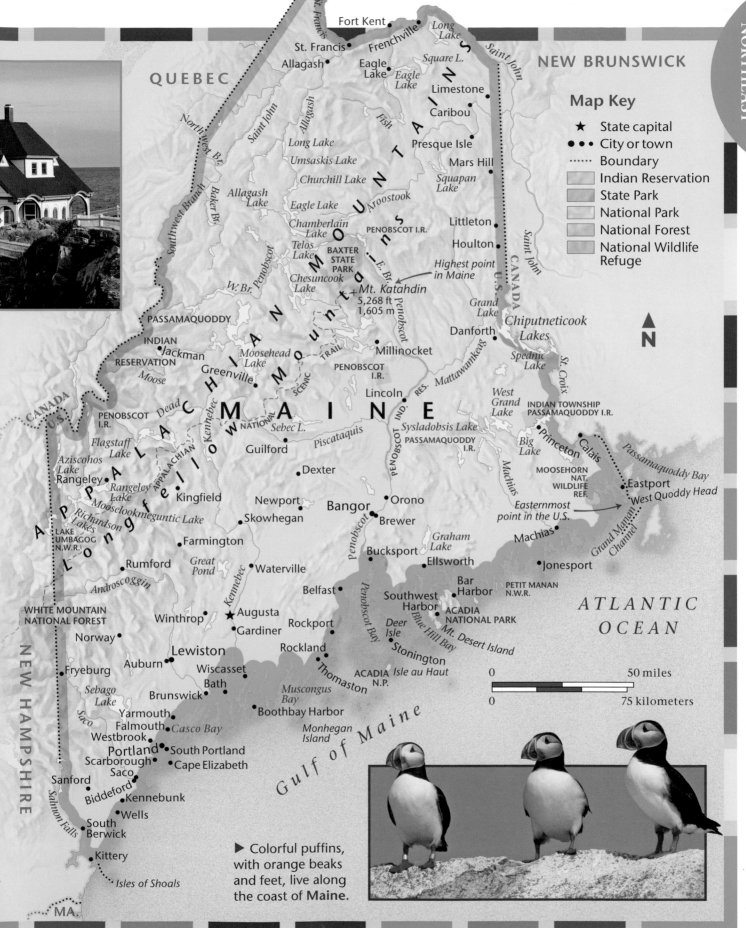

QUEBEC

NEW BRUNSWICK

Fort Kent
St. Francis
Frenchville
Long Lake
Allagash
Eagle Lake
Eagle Lake
Square L.
Saint John
Limestone
Caribou
Presque Isle
Mars Hill
Squapan Lake

Long Lake
Umsaskis Lake
Churchill Lake
Allagash Lake
Eagle Lake
Chamberlain Lake
Telos Lake
Chesuncook Lake
PENOBSCOT I.R.
Littleton
Houlton

North West Br.
Southwest Branch
Saint John
Allagash
Fish
Aroostook

Map Key
★ State capital
• • • City or town
• • • • Boundary
▭ Indian Reservation
▭ State Park
▭ National Park
▭ National Forest
▭ National Wildlife Refuge

Baker Br.

BAXTER STATE PARK
Highest point in Maine
+ Mt. Katahdin
5,268 ft
1,605 m

W. Br. Penobscot

Grand Lake
Danforth
Chiputneticook Lakes

N.E. Br. Penobscot

Saint John
CANADA
U.S.

PASSAMAQUODDY INDIAN RESERVATION
Jackman
Moose
Moosehead Lake
Greenville
PENOBSCOT I.R.
Millinocket
Spednic Lake
St. Croix

CANADA
U.S.
PENOBSCOT I.R.
Dead
Kennebec
MAINE
Lincoln
Mattawamkeag
West Grand Lake
INDIAN TOWNSHIP PASSAMAQUODDY I.R.

APPALACHIAN MOUNTAINS
SCENIC
NATIONAL
TRAIL
Sebec L.
Piscataquis
Sysladobsis Lake
PASSAMAQUODDY I.R.
Big Lake
Princeton
Calais

Flagstaff Lake
Guilford
PENOBSCOT
Machias
MOOSEHORN NAT. WILDLIFE REF.
Passamaquoddy Bay

Azischos Lake
Rangeley
Rangeley Lake
Mooselookmeguntic Lake
Kingfield
Dexter
Newport
Orono
Bangor
Brewer
Eastport
West Quoddy Head
Easternmost point in the U.S.

Richardson Lakes
LAKE UMBAGOG N.W.R.
Farmington
Skowhegan
Graham Lake
Machias

APPALACHIAN
LONGFELLOW
Rumford
Great Pond
Waterville
Bucksport
Ellsworth
Jonesport

Androscoggin
Kennebec
Belfast
Southwest Harbor
Bar Harbor
PETIT MANAN N.W.R.

WHITE MOUNTAIN NATIONAL FOREST
Winthrop
★ Augusta
Gardiner
Rockport
Deer Isle
Blue Hill Bay
Mt. Desert Island
ACADIA NATIONAL PARK
ATLANTIC OCEAN

Norway
Lewiston
Rockland
Penobscot Bay
Stonington

Auburn
Wiscasset
Bath
Thomaston
ACADIA N.P.
Isle au Haut

Fryeburg
Sebago Lake
Brunswick
Muscongus Bay

Saco
Yarmouth
Falmouth
Westbrook
Casco Bay
Boothbay Harbor
Monhegan Island

NEW HAMPSHIRE
Sanford
Portland
Scarborough
Saco
South Portland
Cape Elizabeth

Biddeford
Kennebunk
Salmon Falls
South Berwick
Wells

Kittery
Isles of Shoals

Gulf of Maine

MA

▶ Colorful puffins, with orange beaks and feet, live along the coast of **Maine**.

N

0   50 miles
0   75 kilometers

Maryland

 Land & Water The Appalachian Mountains, Potomac River, and Chesapeake Bay are important land and water features of Maryland.

 Statehood Maryland became the 7th state in 1788.

 People & Places Maryland's population is 5,633,597. Annapolis is the state's capital. The largest city is Baltimore.

 Fun Fact The name of Baltimore's professional football team—the Ravens—may have been inspired by a poem written by the famous American author Edgar Allan Poe, who lived in Baltimore in the mid-1800s.

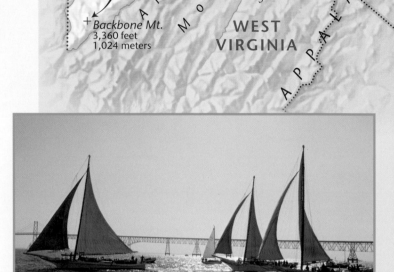

▲ Sailing is a popular pastime on Maryland's **Chesapeake Bay**. In the background, the Bay Bridge stretches 4.3 miles (6.9 km) across the waters of the Bay.

Maryland State Flag

Black-eyed Susan State Flower

Northern (Baltimore) Oriole State Bird

▲ Since the early 1700s, Baltimore, near the upper Chesapeake Bay, has been a major seaport and focus of trade, industry, and immigration.

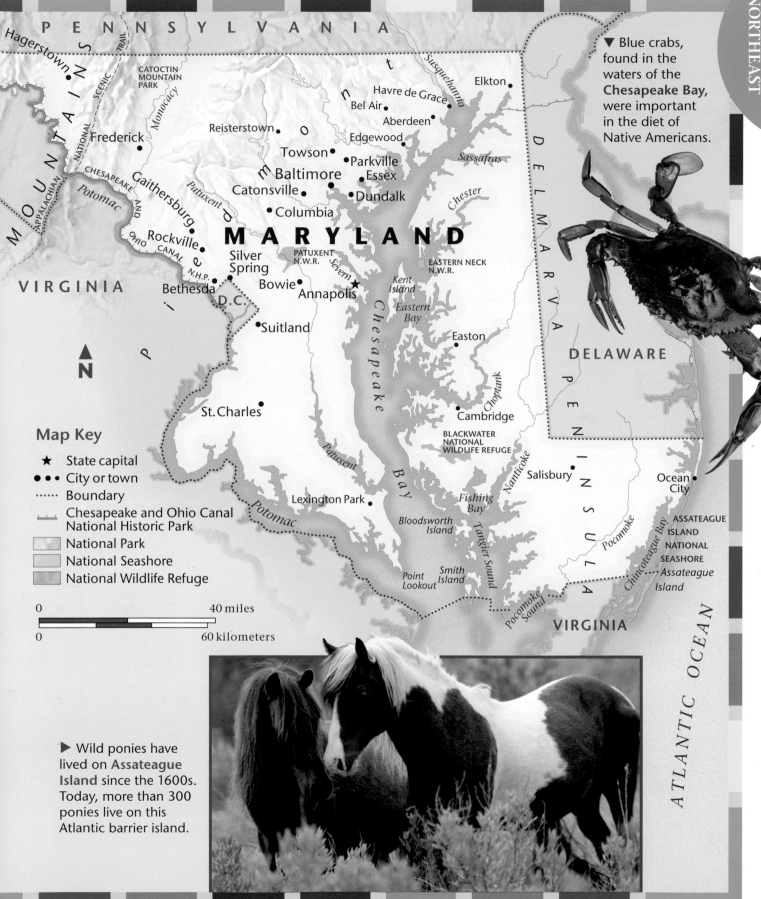

PENNSYLVANIA

Hagerstown

CATOCTIN MOUNTAIN PARK

Elkton

Havre de Grace

Bel Air

Aberdeen

Reisterstown

Frederick

Edgewood

Monocacy

Towson

Parkville

Baltimore

Essex

Sassafras

Catonsville

Dundalk

Chester

Columbia

MARYLAND

Rockville

Patuxent

CHESAPEAKE AND OHIO CANAL

Potomac

Silver Spring

PATUXENT N.W.R.

Severn

EASTERN NECK N.W.R.

VIRGINIA

Bethesda

D.C.

Bowie

Annapolis

Kent Island

DELAWARE

Susquehanna

N.H.P.

Suitland

Eastern Bay

Easton

DELMARVA

Choptank

St. Charles

Cambridge

Chesapeake Bay

BLACKWATER NATIONAL WILDLIFE REFUGE

PENINSULA

Salisbury

Ocean City

Patuxent

ASSATEAGUE ISLAND NATIONAL SEASHORE

Lexington Park

Potomac

Fishing Bay

Nanticoke

Pocomoke

Chincoteague Bay

Assateague Island

Bloodsworth Island

Tangier Sound

Point Lookout

Smith Island

VIRGINIA

Pocomoke Sound

ATLANTIC OCEAN

Map Key

★ State capital

●●● City or town

········ Boundary

Chesapeake and Ohio Canal National Historic Park

National Park

National Seashore

National Wildlife Refuge

0 ——— 40 miles

0 ——— 60 kilometers

▼ Blue crabs, found in the waters of the **Chesapeake Bay**, were important in the diet of Native Americans.

▶ Wild ponies have lived on **Assateague Island** since the 1600s. Today, more than 300 ponies live on this Atlantic barrier island.

Massachusetts

Land & Water The Berkshire Mountains, Cape Cod, and Nantucket Sound are important land and water features of Massachusetts.

Statehood Massachusetts became the 6th state in 1788.

People & Places Massachusetts's population is 6,497,967. Boston is the state capital and the largest city.

Fun Fact In 1891, James Naismith invented the game of basketball as a form of physical activity. Today, the Basketball Hall of Fame is located in Springfield in his honor.

▲ Fenway Park in **Boston** is home to the Red Sox major league baseball team. The park was named for a Boston neighborhood known as the Fens.

▼ Cranberries, grown in fields called bogs, are Massachusetts's largest agricultural crop, employing more than 5,000 people. An annual cranberry harvest festival is held in **Wareham**.

Massachusetts State Flag

Chickadee State Bird

Mayflower State Flower

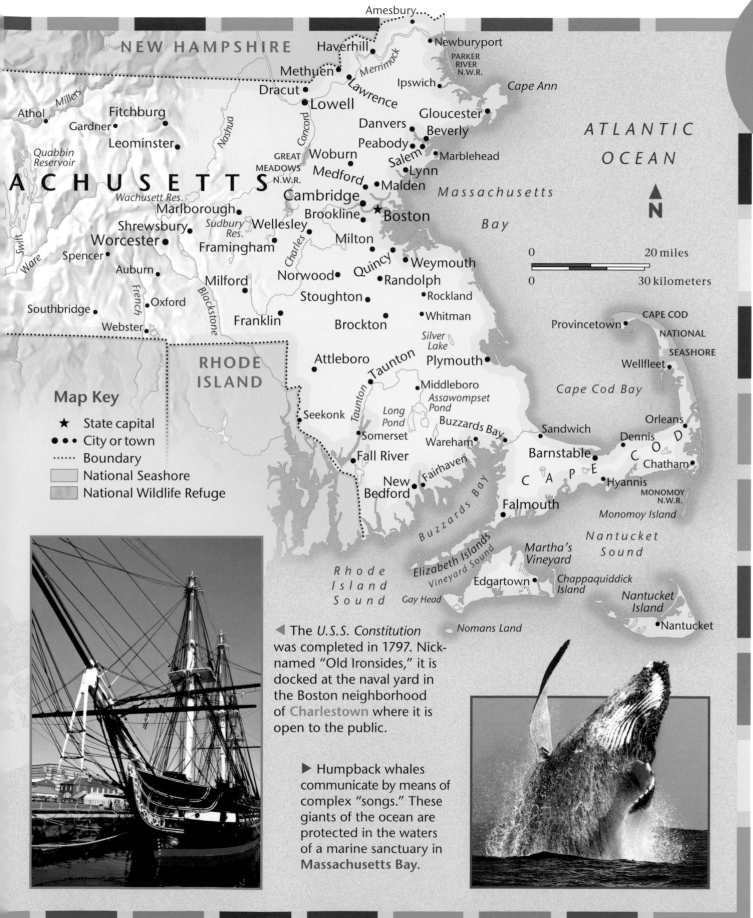

NEW HAMPSHIRE

ATLANTIC OCEAN

N

Amesbury
Haverhill
Methuen
Dracut
Lawrence
Lowell
Ipswich
Newburyport
PARKER RIVER N.W.R.
Cape Ann

Athol
Gardner
Fitchburg
Leominster
Millers
Nashua
Danvers
Peabody
Woburn
Gloucester
Beverly
Salem
Marblehead

Quabbin Reservoir
MASSACHUSETTS
Wachusett Res.
GREAT MEADOWS N.W.R.
Medford
Malden
Cambridge
Lynn
Massachusetts Bay

Marlborough
Brookline
★ Boston

Shrewsbury
Wellesley
Milton
Sudbury Res.
Worcester
Framingham
Charles
Swift
Ware
Spencer
Auburn
Norwood
Quincy
Weymouth
Randolph
Milford
French
Stoughton
Rockland
0   20 miles
0   30 kilometers

Southbridge
Oxford
Blackstone
Franklin
Brockton
Whitman
Provincetown
CAPE COD NATIONAL SEASHORE
Wellfleet
Webster

Silver Lake

RHODE ISLAND

Attleboro
Taunton
Taunton
Plymouth
Cape Cod Bay

Middleboro
Assawompset Pond
Orleans

Map Key

★ State capital
••• City or town
···· Boundary
⬜ National Seashore
⬜ National Wildlife Refuge

Seekonk
Long Pond
Buzzards Bay
Sandwich
Dennis
CAPE
COD
Somerset
Wareham
Barnstable
Chatham
Fall River
Fairhaven
CAPE
Hyannis
MONOMOY N.W.R.
New Bedford
Buzzards Bay
Falmouth
Monomoy Island

Rhode Island Sound
Elizabeth Islands
Vineyard Sound
Martha's Vineyard
Nantucket Sound

Edgartown
Chappaquiddick Island
Nantucket Island
Gay Head
Nantucket
Nomans Land

◀ The *U.S.S. Constitution* was completed in 1797. Nicknamed "Old Ironsides," it is docked at the naval yard in the Boston neighborhood of Charlestown where it is open to the public.

▶ Humpback whales communicate by means of complex "songs." These giants of the ocean are protected in the waters of a marine sanctuary in **Massachusetts Bay.**

New Hampshire

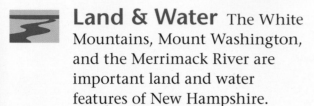

Land & Water The White Mountains, Mount Washington, and the Merrimack River are important land and water features of New Hampshire.

Statehood New Hampshire became the 9th state in 1788.

People & Places New Hampshire's population is 1,315,809. Concord is the state capital. The largest city is Manchester.

Fun Fact The first potato grown in the United States was planted in 1719 in Londonderry on the Common Field, now known simply as the Commons.

▲ A golden dome topped by a war eagle rises above New Hampshire's State House in **Concord**. The pale granite building was completed in 1819.

◄ Bitter cold and heavy snow are common in the White Mountains of New Hampshire, where snow tubing and skiing are popular winter sports.

▼ **Mount Washington** rises above trees rich with autumn colors. But soon winter will arrive, bringing some of the most extreme weather in the world.

New Hampshire State Flag

Purple Lilac State Flower

Purple Finch State Bird

Map Key

★ State capital
•‒• City or town
····· Boundary
State Park
National Forest
National Wildlife Refuge

QUEBEC

Third L.
First Connecticut Lake
Second Lake
Lake Francis

CANADA
U.S.

• Colebrook

LAKE UMBAGOG N.W.R.

Umbagog Lake

• North Stratford

Androscoggin

Upper Ammonoosuc

• Groveton

W H I T E

• Lancaster

• Berlin

Moore Reservoir

A P P A L A C H I A N   M O U N T A I N

TRAIL

• Littleton

Ammonoosuc

+ Mt. Washington
6,288 ft 1,917 m

• Lisbon

FRANCONIA NOTCH S.P.

N A T I O N A L   M t s.

CRAWFORD NOTCH S.P.

Saco

SCENIC

Highest point in New Hampshire

• Haverhill

White

F O R E S T

VERMONT

M O U N T A I N S

N E W

• Orford

• Conway

Conway Lake

H A M P S H I R E

Baker

Squam Lake

Bearcamp

Ossipee

• Ossipee Lake

• Center Sandwich

MAINE

Newfound Lake

• Hanover

Lake Wentworth

• Lebanon

Mascoma Lake

• Enfield

• Bristol

Perquawsset

Lake Winnipesaukee

• Laconia

Merrymeeting Lake

Winnipesaukee

Crystal Lake

Winnisquam Lake

Sunapee Lake

• New London

• Franklin

Winnipesaukee

• Farmington

Sugar

Suncook Lakes

Cocheco

Salmon Falls

• Claremont

MT. SUNAPEE S.P.

Merrimack

• Pittsfield

• Rochester

• Somersworth

• Charlestown

• Contoocook

Bow Lake

• Dover

• Hillsboro

★ Concord

Suncook

• Durham

• Suncook

Piscataqua

Highland Lake

• Walpole

• Antrim

Contoocook

• Raymond

Lamprey

Great Bay

• Portsmouth

Surry Mt. Lake

Nubanusit Lake

• Manchester

• Exeter

Massabesic Lake

• Hampton

Isles of Shoals

WAPACK N.W.R.

• Londonderry

• Keene

• Derry

• Peterborough

• Merrimack

PISGAH S.P.

Southegan

• Milford

• Atkinson

Ashuelot

• Hinsdale

• Winchester

• New Ipswich

• Salem

Merrimack

ATLANTIC OCEAN

• Nashua

Connecticut

MASSACHUSETTS

▲ A black bear cub clings to the trunk of a tree in a **New Hampshire** forest.

N

0 — 20 miles
0 — 30 kilometers

New Jersey

Land & Water The Kittatinny Mountains, Cape May, and the Delaware River are important land and water features in New Jersey.

Statehood New Jersey became the 3rd state in 1787.

People & Places New Jersey's population is 8,682,661. Trenton is the state capital. The largest city is Newark.

Fun Fact The first dinosaur skeleton found in North America was excavated at Haddonfield in 1858. It was named Hadrosaurus in honor of its discovery site.

▲ Sandy beaches on the Atlantic coast of **New Jersey** attract vacationers from near and far. Roller coasters are just one of the exciting rides in amusement parks along the shore.

◄ Street names, such as Boardwalk and Park Place, in the popular board game of Monopoly are taken from actual street names in Atlantic City.

New Jersey State Flag

▼ The skylines of **Jersey City** (left) and New York City (in the distance at right) glow in the evening light. Jersey City, second largest city in the state, is home to many large corporations.

America Goldfinch State Bird

Violet State Flower

▲ Victorian-style houses line a street in **Cape May.** The town is a national historic landmark and the country's oldest seashore resort.

▲ New Jersey, known as the **Garden State,** is a leading producer of fresh fruits and vegetables.

Southern Jersey
Tomatoes
$2.50

NEW YORK

High Point
1,803 ft
550 m
Highest point
in New Jersey

Delaware

APPALACHIAN

DELAWARE WATER GAP N.R.A.

NATIONAL

SCENIC TRAIL

Kittatinny Mountains

Highland Lakes
Ringwood
Wanaque Reservoir
Ramsey
Newton
Wanaque
Sparta
Ridgewood
Paramus
Lake
Hopatcong
Wayne
Hackensack
Hopatcong
Paterson
Dover
Clifton
Passaic
Hackettstown
Morristown
MORRISTOWN
N.H.P.
Newark
Jersey City
Phillipsburg
Bernardsville
GREAT
SWAMP
N.W.R.
Berkeley Heights
Elizabeth
Bayonne
High Bridge
Round
Valley Res.
Somerville
Raritan
Lower Bay
Flemington
Edison
Sandy Hook
New Brunswick
Sandy Hook
Bay
Delaware & Raritan Canal
East
Brunswick
GATEWAY
N.R.A.
N E W
Red Bank
Princeton
Eatontown
Long
Branch
Mercerville
Freehold
Asbury
Park
Trenton
Neptune
White Horse
PENNSYLVANIA
J E R S E Y
Point Pleasant
Burlington
Lakewood
Willingboro
Mount Holly
Toms River
Seaside
Heights
Camden
Pennsauken
Cherry Hill
Woodbury
P I N E   B A R R E N S
Lindenwold
Long Beach
Island
Glassboro
Ship Bottom
DELAWARE
Delaware
Hammonton
Little Egg Harbor
Salem
Pennsville
Beach Haven
SUPAWNA MEADOWS
N.W.R.
Maurice
Mullica
Great
Bay
Vineland
Great Egg Harbor
Pleasantville
Brigantine
Bridgeton
Cohansey
Millville
Atlantic City
Somers Point
Ventnor City
Tuckahoe
Ocean City

Map Key
★ State capital
••• City or town
····· Boundary
National Historic Park
National Recreation Area
National Wildlife Refuge

Woodbine

CAPE MAY N.W.R.

Cape May Court House
Villas
CAPE
MAY
Delaware
Bay
Wildwood

Cape May

A T L A N T I C
O C E A N

N

0   20 miles
0   30 kilometers

Passaic
Hudson
Ellis Island

Manalapan
Toms

Barnegat Bay

E. B. FORSYTHE N.W.R.

Musconetcong

The Northeast

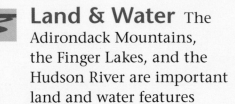

New York

Land & Water The Adirondack Mountains, the Finger Lakes, and the Hudson River are important land and water features of New York.

Statehood New York became the 11th state in 1788.

People & Places New York's population is 19,490,297. Albany is the state capital. The largest city is New York City.

Fun Fact The Erie Canal, built in the 1820s between Albany and Buffalo, allowed ships to travel from the Atlantic Ocean to the Great Lakes. The canal helped New York City become a major trading center.

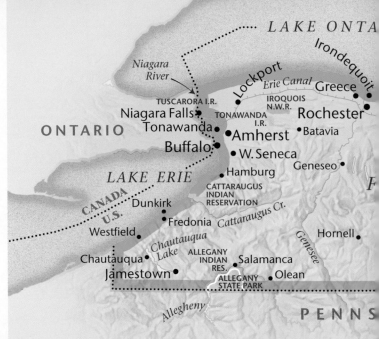

LAKE ONTA

Niagara River

Irondequoit

Lockport

Erie Canal

Greece

TUSCARORA I.R.

IROQUOIS N.W.R.

Niagara Falls

TONAWANDA I.R.

Rochester

ONTARIO

Tonawanda

Amherst

Batavia

Buffalo

W. Seneca

CANADA

U.S.

LAKE ERIE

Hamburg

Geneseo

CATTARAUGUS INDIAN RESERVATION

Dunkirk

Cattaraugus Cr.

Fredonia

Genesee

Hornell

Westfield

Chautauqua Lake

ALLEGANY INDIAN RES.

Salamanca

Chautauqua

Jamestown

ALLEGANY STATE PARK

Olean

Allegheny

PENNS

New York State Flag

Eastern Bluebird State Bird

Rose State Flower

◄ Fresh juicy apples are on display at a roadside stand near Chautauqua. New York is the second largest producer of apples in the U.S.

▲ Standing in **New York Harbor**, the Statue of Liberty, a gift from the people of France, is a symbol of freedom and democracy.

◄ Once seriously polluted, the **Gowanus Canal** in New York City's borough of Brooklyn has been undergoing cleaning efforts. Here, people canoe and enjoy the view from the water.

QUEBEC

CANADA
U.S.

ONTARIO

St. Lawrence

Thousand Islands

RIO

Massena
ST. REGIS I.R.
Malone
Potsdam
Plattsburgh
Ogdensburg

Lake Champlain

Lake Placid

Raquette

A d i r o n d a c k

Mt. Marcy +
5,344 ft
1,629 m

Highest point in New York

Ticonderoga

Watertown

ADIRONDACK

M o u n t a i n s

PARK

Lake George

Black

Hudson

VERMONT

Oswego
Fulton
Oswego

Oneida Lake

Rome
Utica
Oneida

Warrensburg

Glens Falls

Great Sacandaga Lake

Saratoga Springs
Gloversville

Canandaigua
Geneva
MONTEZUMA N.W.R.
Seneca Falls
Auburn
Syracuse
ONONDAGA INDIAN RESERVATION

Mohawk

Amsterdam

Schenectady

Seneca Lake
nger Lakes
Cayuga Lake
Cortland
Cooperstown

MOUNTAINS

Troy

Albany ★

MASSACHUSETTS

N E W   Y O R K

Keuka Lake
FINGER LAKES N.F.
Ithaca

Oneonta

Susquehanna

Taconic Ranges

Bath
Watkins Glen
Corning
Elmira
Endwell
Binghamton

Chemung

A P P A L A C H I A N

W. Br. Delaware
E. Branch

Catskill Mountains

CATSKILL PARK

Slide Mt. +
4,180 ft
1,274 m

Catskill
Hudson

Kingston

Hudson

CONNECTICUT

LVANIA

Susquehanna

Delaware

New Paltz

Beacon

Poughkeepsie

TRAIL

SCENIC

RHODE ISLAND

Newburgh

Middletown
Port Jervis

Peekskill

New City

NATIONAL

APPALACHIAN

Spring Valley

Tarrytown
White Plains

New Rochelle

Block Island Sound

Long Island Sound

Montauk Point

Yonkers

Huntington

Centereach

East Hampton
Southampton

New York

Brentwood

Ellis Island

Levittown

FIRE ISLAND NATIONAL SEASHORE

Long Island

ATLANTIC OCEAN

NEW JERSEY

Staten Island

GATEWAY N.R.A.

Freeport

Long Beach

Map Key

★ State capital
• • • City or town
· · · · · Boundary
Indian Reservation
State Park
National Recreation Area
National Seashore
National Forest
National Wildlife Refuge

0   50 miles
0   75 kilometers

N

Pennsylvania

Land & Water The Allegheny Mountains, the Pocono Mountains, and the Susquehanna River are important land and water features of Pennsylvania.

Statehood Pennsylvania became the 2nd state in 1787.

People & Places Pennsylvania's population is 12,448,279. Harrisburg is the state capital. The largest city is Philadelphia.

Fun Fact The town of Hershey is known as the Chocolate Capital of the World. The Hershey Company exports its chocolate candies to more than 90 countries around the world.

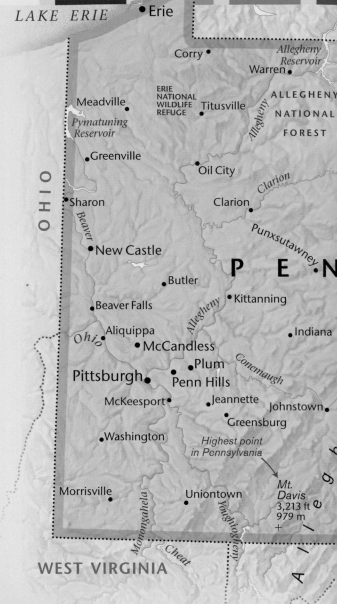

LAKE ERIE • Erie

OHIO

Corry •
Warren •
Allegheny Reservoir

Meadville •
ERIE NATIONAL WILDLIFE REFUGE
Titusville •
ALLEGHENY NATIONAL FOREST

Pymatuning Reservoir

• Greenville

Oil City •

• Sharon

Clarion •

Beaver

Punxsutawney

P • E • N

• New Castle

• Butler

• Kittanning

Beaver Falls •

Allegheny

• Indiana

Aliquippa •
• McCandless

Ohio

• Plum

Conemaugh

Pittsburgh
• Penn Hills

McKeesport •
• Jeannette
Johnstown •

• Greensburg

• Washington

Highest point in Pennsylvania

Morrisville •

Monongahela
Cheat

• Uniontown

Youghiogheny

Mt. Davis
3,213 ft
979 m

Allegheny

WEST VIRGINIA

Map Key

★ State capital
●●● City or town
······ Boundary
☐ National Recreation Area
☐ National Forest
☐ National Wildlife Refuge

Pennsylvania State Flag

Mountain Laurel State Flower

Ruffed Grouse State Bird

APPALACHIAN TRAIL

◄ The **Appalachian Trail** stretches across more than 2,000 miles (3,200 km) from Maine to Georgia. The trail passes through 14 states, including Pennsylvania.

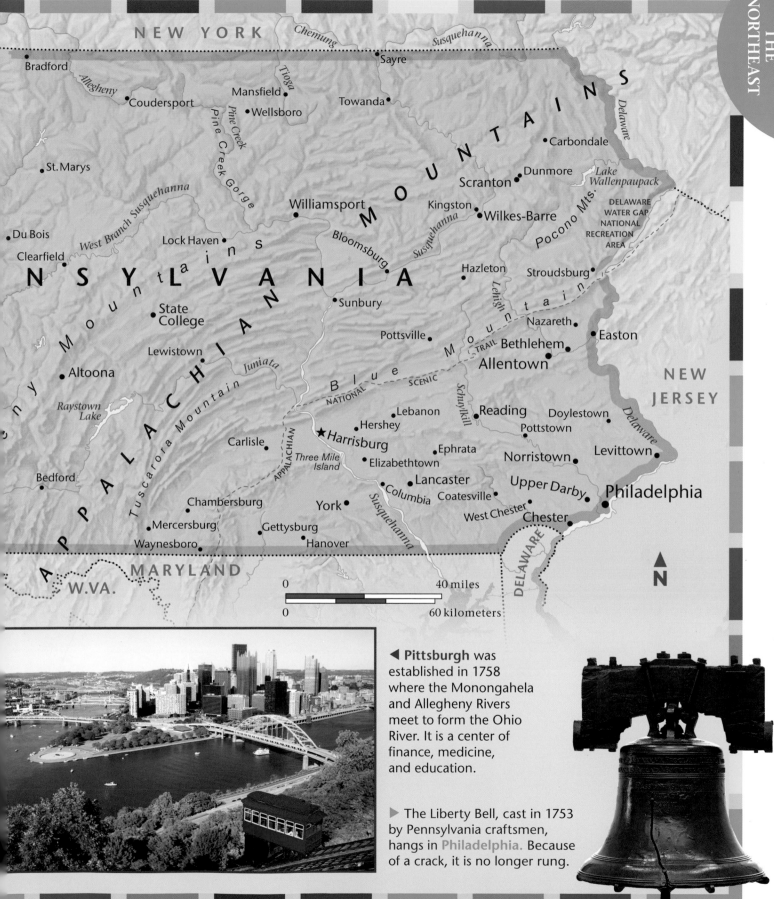

NEW YORK

Chemung

Susquehanna

Bradford

Allegheny

Sayre

Coudersport

Mansfield

Towanda

Wellsboro

Tioga

Pine Creek

Carbondale

St. Marys

Pine Creek Gorge

Dunmore

Lake Wallenpaupack

Scranton

Delaware

Williamsport

Kingston

Wilkes-Barre

M O U N T A I N S

West Branch Susquehanna

Du Bois

Lock Haven

Bloomsburg

Susquehanna

Pocono Mts.

DELAWARE WATER GAP NATIONAL RECREATION AREA

Clearfield

Hazleton

Stroudsburg

N S Y L V A N I A

Sunbury

Lehigh

M o u n t a i n

Mountains

State College

Pottsville

Nazareth

Easton

Lewistown

Blue

Mountain

TRAIL

Bethlehem

Altoona

Juniata

NATIONAL

SCENIC

Allentown

NEW JERSEY

Raystown Lake

Lebanon

Schuylkill

Reading

Doylestown

Delaware

A P P A L A C H I A N

Tuscarora Mountain

Carlisle

Hershey

Pottstown

Levittown

APPALACHIAN

★ Harrisburg

Ephrata

Norristown

Bedford

Three Mile Island

Elizabethtown

Lancaster

Upper Darby

Philadelphia

Chambersburg

York

Columbia

Coatesville

West Chester

Chester

Mercersburg

Gettysburg

Susquehanna

Waynesboro

Hanover

DELAWARE

N

MARYLAND

W. VA.

0   40 miles

0   60 kilometers

◀ **Pittsburgh** was established in 1758 where the Monongahela and Allegheny Rivers meet to form the Ohio River. It is a center of finance, medicine, and education.

▶ The Liberty Bell, cast in 1753 by Pennsylvania craftsmen, hangs in Philadelphia. Because of a crack, it is no longer rung.

Rhode Island

Land & Water Block Island and Narragansett Bay, with its many islands, are important land and water features of Rhode Island.

Statehood Rhode Island became the 13th state in 1790.

People & Places Rhode Island's population is 1,050,788. Providence is the state capital and the largest city.

Fun Fact Rhode Island is the smallest state in size in the United States. It measures just 48 miles from north to south and 37 miles from east to west.

Rhode Island State Flag

Violet State Flower

Rhode Island Red State Bird

▲ Sailing is a popular sport in Rhode Island. This boat is in full sail on a late summer day on Narragansett Bay.

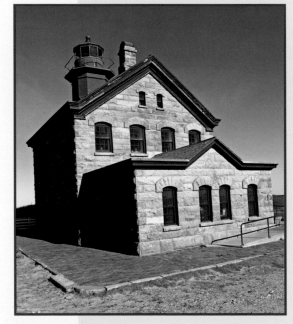

◄ The North Lighthouse on the northern tip of **Block Island** still warns ships of dangerous waters. The building, constructed in 1867, is not a typical lighthouse design.

▼ Rhode Island has cold, snowy winters. Skaters bundled in warm clothing enjoy ice skating on the City Center public rink in Providence.

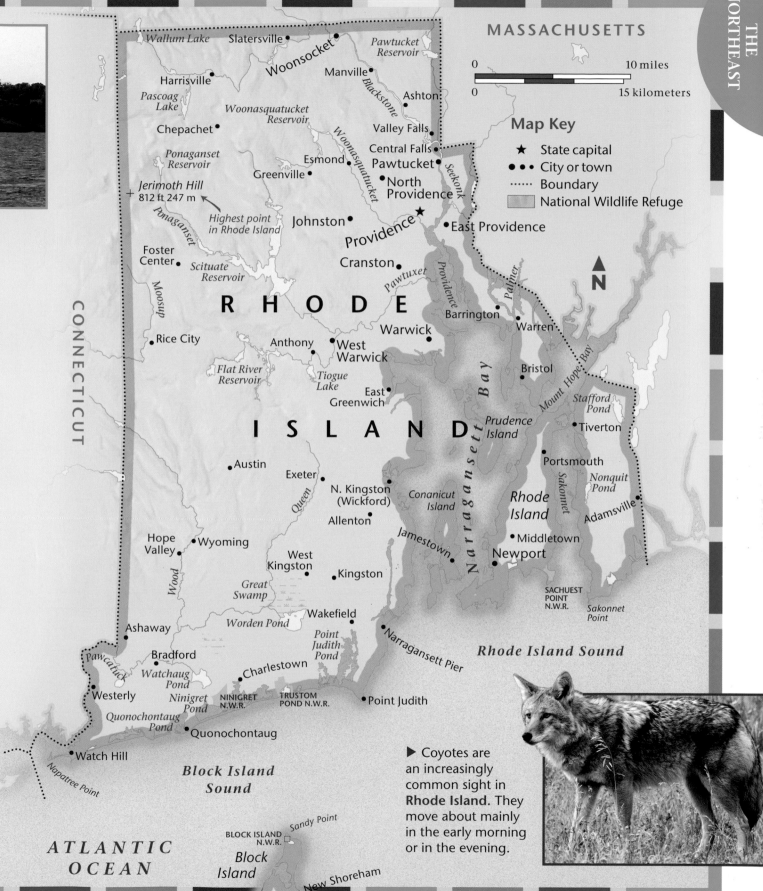

MASSACHUSETTS

Wallum Lake Slatersville Woonsocket *Pawtucket Reservoir*

Harrisville Manville Ashton

Pascoag Lake *Woonasquatucket Reservoir* *Blackstone*

Chepachet Valley Falls

Ponaganset Reservoir Esmond Central Falls *Woonasquatucket* Pawtucket *Seekonk*

Greenville North Providence

Jerimoth Hill *Ponaganset* Johnston

+ 812 ft 247 m Providence East Providence

Highest point in Rhode Island

Foster Center Cranston *Pawtuxet*

Scituate Reservoir **R H O D E** *Providence*

Moosup Barrington *Palmer* Warren

Rice City Warwick Bristol *Mount Hope Bay* *Stafford Pond*

Anthony West Warwick *Narragansett Bay*

I S L A N D Tiverton

Flat River Reservoir *Tiogue Lake* East Greenwich Prudence Island

Prudence Island *Sakonnet* Portsmouth *Nonquit Pond*

Austin Exeter N. Kingston (Wickford) *Conanicut Island* **Rhode Island** Adamsville

Queen Allenton Jamestown Middletown

Hope Valley Wyoming West Kingston Kingston Newport

Wood *Great Swamp* Wakefield **SACHUEST POINT N.W.R.** *Sakonnet Point*

Worden Pond Point Judith Pond Narragansett Pier

Ashaway *Rhode Island Sound*

Pawcatuck Bradford Charlestown

Watchaug Pond Westerly *Ninigret Pond* **NINIGRET N.W.R.** **TRUSTOM POND N.W.R.** Point Judith

Quonochontaug Pond Quonochontaug

Watch Hill *Napatree Point* *Block Island Sound*

ATLANTIC OCEAN *Sandy Point* **BLOCK ISLAND N.W.R.** *Block Island* New Shoreham

CONNECTICUT

Map Key

★ State capital
●●● City or town
···· Boundary
▨ National Wildlife Refuge

0 ——— 10 miles
0 ——— 15 kilometers

N

► Coyotes are an increasingly common sight in **Rhode Island.** They move about mainly in the early morning or in the evening.

The Northeast

Vermont

Land & Water The Green Mountains, Lake Champlain, and the Connecticut River are important land and water features of Vermont.

Statehood Vermont became the 14th state in 1791.

People & Places Vermont's population is 621,270. Montpelier is the state capital. The largest city is Burlington.

Fun Fact From the end of the Revolutionary War until 1791, Vermont was an independent republic with its own government and money. It even thought about uniting with Canada.

▲ Vermont ice cream is famous worldwide. The headquarters of Ben & Jerry's in **Burlington** is the number one tourist attraction in the state.

Vermont State Flag

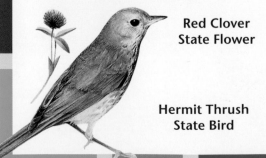

Red Clover State Flower

Hermit Thrush State Bird

▲ People collect the sap of maple trees, which is boiled to make maple sugar and syrup. Maple production is celebrated each year at a festival in Tunbridge.

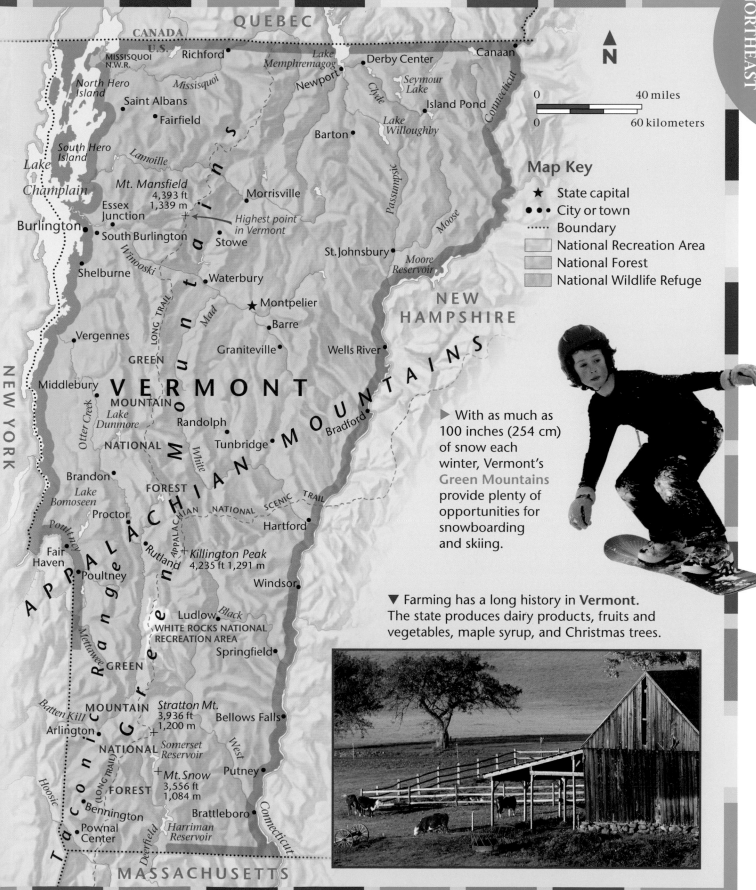

QUEBEC

CANADA
U.S.

MISSISQUOI
N.W.R.

Richford

Lake
Memphremagog

Derby Center

Canaan

Newport

Seymour
Lake

Island Pond

Connecticut

N

0   40 miles
0   60 kilometers

North Hero
Island

Missisquoi

Saint Albans

Fairfield

Barton

Lake
Willoughby

South Hero
Island

Lake
Champlain

Lamoille

Clyde

Passumpsic

Map Key

★ State capital
• • • City or town
· · · · · Boundary
National Recreation Area
National Forest
National Wildlife Refuge

Mt. Mansfield
4,393 ft
1,339 m

Morrisville

Burlington

Essex
Junction

South Burlington

Stowe

Highest point
in Vermont

Moose

St. Johnsbury

Winooski

Shelburne

Waterbury

Moore
Reservoir

NEW
HAMPSHIRE

Vergennes

Mad

Montpelier

GREEN

Barre

Graniteville

Wells River

Middlebury

VERMONT

LONG TRAIL

MOUNTAIN

Lake
Dunmore

Randolph

Otter Creek

NATIONAL

Tunbridge

White

Bradford

▶ With as much as
100 inches (254 cm)
of snow each
winter, Vermont's
Green Mountains
provide plenty of
opportunities for
snowboarding
and skiing.

Brandon

Lake
Bomoseen

Proctor

FOREST

NATIONAL SCENIC TRAIL

APPALACHIAN

Hartford

Poultney

Rutland

Killington Peak
4,235 ft 1,291 m

Fair
Haven

Poultney

Windsor

Ludlow

Black

WHITE ROCKS NATIONAL
RECREATION AREA

Mettawee

Springfield

▼ Farming has a long history in Vermont.
The state produces dairy products, fruits and
vegetables, maple syrup, and Christmas trees.

GREEN

Batten Kill

MOUNTAIN

Stratton Mt.
3,936 ft
1,200 m

Bellows Falls

Arlington

Somerset
Reservoir

West

Putney

NATIONAL

Mt. Snow
3,556 ft
1,084 m

Hoosic

(LONG TRAIL)

FOREST

Bennington

Brattleboro

Pownal
Center

Deerfield

Harriman
Reservoir

Connecticut

MASSACHUSETTS

NEW YORK

APPALACHIAN Range

Taconic

Green Mountains

The Southeast

The Southeast region of the United States is full of variety, both in its landscape and in its history. The Appalachian Mountains are old and worn down. The coastal margins are marked by barrier islands and wetlands. And in the western part of the region, the Mississippi River flows out through a broad delta. The region, with roots in agriculture, suffered great destruction during the Civil War, but today it is a part of the Sunbelt, where cities are growing rapidly and the economy is shifting to high-tech industries.

Live oak trees, some hundreds of years old, form a natural arch across a country road in Georgia. These trees, draped in Spanish moss, are common in the coastal Southeast. Flamingoes are a familiar sight in parks in Florida.

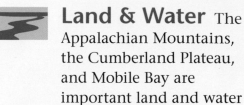

Alabama

Land & Water The Appalachian Mountains, the Cumberland Plateau, and Mobile Bay are important land and water features of Alabama.

Statehood Alabama became the 22nd state in 1819.

People & Places Alabama's population is 4,661,900. Montgomery is the state capital. The largest city is Birmingham.

Fun Fact The world's youngest college graduate earned a bachelor's degree in anthropology from the University of South Alabama when he was just 10 years and four months old.

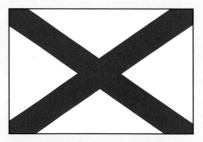
Alabama State Flag

Northern Flicker State Bird

Camellia State Flower

▲ Southern Alabama has a narrow coastline fronting the Gulf of Mexico. The beach resort of **Gulf Shores** is a popular tourist destination.

▲ A welder repairs a boat in **Bayou La Batre** on Alabama's Gulf coast. The town is a center for shipbuilding and seafood processing.

▼ This old railroad bridge, built in 1839, was a toll bridge across the **Tennessee River.** Today it is a pedestrian bridge.

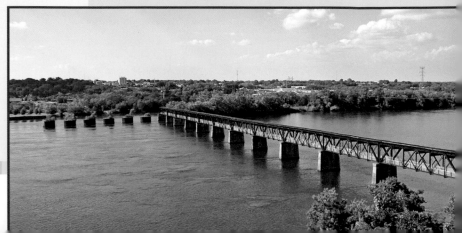

Map Key

★ State capital
• • • City or town
..... Boundary

National Preserve
National Forest
National Wildlife Refuge

TENNESSEE

Pickwick Lake
Wilson Lake
Florence
Athens
Huntsville
Muscle Shoals
Madison
Scottsboro
Tennessee
Wheeler Lake
Decatur
WHEELER N.W.R.
Guntersville Lake
LITTLE RIVER CANYON NATIONAL PRESERVE
Russellville
Hartselle
Guntersville
Fort Payne

BANKHEAD
Cullman
Albertville
Weiss Lake

NATIONAL
Mulberry Fork
Locust Fork
Gadsden
APPALACHIAN MTS.

FOREST
Winfield
Lewis Smith Lake
Jasper
Warrior
Center Point
Anniston
TALLADEGA

Birmingham
Cheaha Mt. 2,407 ft 734 m
NATIONAL
Hueytown
Homewood
Talladega
Chattahoochee
Bessemer
Hoover
FOREST
Highest point in Alabama
GEORGIA

Tuscaloosa
Alabaster
Coosa
Roanoke

Sipsey
Sylacauga

Black Warrior
TALLADEGA
Alexander City
West Point Lake

York
NATIONAL
Clanton
Lake Martin
Valley

FOREST
Opelika

A L A B A M A
Millbrook
Auburn

Demopolis
Cahaba
Selma
Prattville
Tallapoosa
TUSKEGEE NAT. FOR.

Tombigbee
B l a c k
Phenix City

Tuskegee

Montgomery
Union Springs
EUFAULA N.W.R.

B e l t
Alabama

William "Bill" Dannelly Reservoir

CHOCTAW N.W.R.
Thomasville
Greenville
Eufaula

Tombigbee
Troy
Walter F. George Reservoir

Monroeville
Conecuh
Abbeville

Evergreen
Ozark
Pea

Alabama
Andalusia
Enterprise
Choctawhatchee
Dothan

Saraland
Brewton
CONECUH NATIONAL FOREST
Geneva

Prichard
Atmore
Conecuh

Mobile
Tensaw

Mobile
Perdido
0 50 miles
0 75 kilometers

Daphne
Fairhope
N

Bayou La Batre
Mobile Bay

Mississippi Sound
Dauphin Island
Gulf Shores
Intracoastal Waterway
FLORIDA

GULF OF MEXICO

MISSISSIPPI

▲ The bobwhite quail is common throughout Alabama. They build their nests on the ground and live on a diet of seeds.

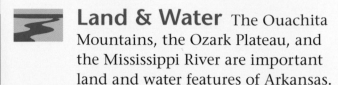

The Southeast

Arkansas

Land & Water The Ouachita Mountains, the Ozark Plateau, and the Mississippi River are important land and water features of Arkansas.

Statehood Arkansas became the 25th state in 1836.

People & Places Arkansas's population is 2,855,390. Little Rock is the state capital and the largest city.

Fun Fact Crater of Diamonds State Park near Murfreesboro yielded the largest natural diamond ever found in the United States in 1924. The stone, called "Uncle Sam," weighed more than 40 carats.

◄ A student with his laptop computer sits on the monument to Confederate soldiers on the state capitol grounds in **Little Rock.**

Arkansas State Flag

Apple Blossom State Flower

Mockingbird State Bird

▲ A farmer in **eastern Arkansas** checks the progress of his rice crop. The state is a leading producer of rice.

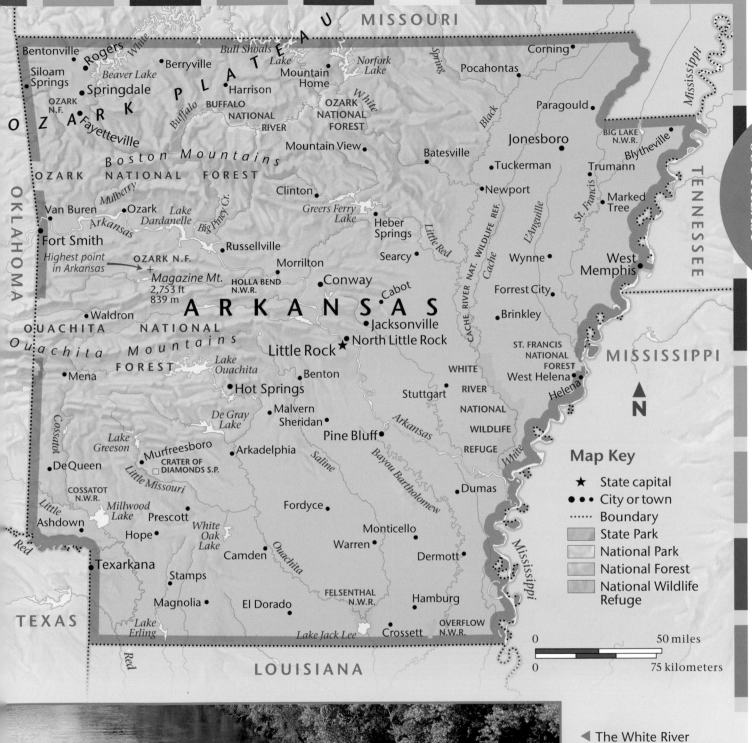

MISSOURI

Bentonville
Rogers
Siloam Springs
Berryville
Springdale
Harrison
OZARK N.F.
Fayetteville

O Z A R K   P L A T E A U

White
Bull Shoals Lake
Beaver Lake
Mountain Home
Norfork Lake
Spring
Corning
Pocahontas
Paragould

Boston Mountains

Buffalo
BUFFALO NATIONAL RIVER
OZARK NATIONAL FOREST
White
Mountain View

OZARK NATIONAL FOREST

Van Buren
Ozark
Mulberry
Lake Dardanelle
Big Piney Cr.
Clinton
Greers Ferry Lake
Heber Springs

Batesville
Tuckerman
Newport
Jonesboro
BIG LAKE N.W.R.
Blytheville
Trumann
Marked Tree

Arkansas
Fort Smith
Russellville
Morrilton

Black
L'Anguille
St. Francis
Little Red
Searcy

Wynne
West Memphis

Highest point in Arkansas
OZARK N.F.
Magazine Mt.
2,753 ft
839 m
HOLLA BEND N.W.R.
Conway
Cabot

Forrest City

Waldron

A R K A N S A S

Jacksonville
North Little Rock
Little Rock ★

Brinkley

CACHE RIVER NAT. WILDLIFE REF.
Cache
ST. FRANCIS NATIONAL FOREST
West Helena
Helena

O U A C H I T A   N A T I O N A L
Ouachita Mountains
FOREST

Lake Ouachita
Benton
Hot Springs

Stuttgart

WHITE
RIVER
NATIONAL
WILDLIFE
REFUGE

MISSISSIPPI

N

Mena

De Gray Lake
Malvern
Sheridan
Pine Bluff

Arkansas
White

Cossatot
Lake Greeson
Murfreesboro
CRATER OF DIAMONDS S.P.
Arkadelphia

Saline

Bayou Bartholomew

Map Key

★ State capital
••• City or town
••••• Boundary
State Park
National Park
National Forest
National Wildlife Refuge

DeQueen
Little Missouri
COSSATOT N.W.R.
Millwood Lake
Prescott
White Oak Lake
Fordyce

Dumas

Ashdown
Hope
Warren
Monticello
Dermott

Little
Red

Texarkana
Stamps
Camden
Ouachita

Hamburg

TEXAS

Magnolia
El Dorado
FELSENTHAL N.W.R.

Lake Erling
Lake Jack Lee
Crossett
OVERFLOW N.W.R.

Mississippi

0   50 miles
0   75 kilometers

Red
LOUISIANA

OKLAHOMA

TENNESSEE

◀ The White River flows through the Ozark Plateau. Its cold water is a perfect habitat for trout, a popular sport fish.

Florida

Land & Water
The Florida Keys, the Everglades, and Lake Okeechobee are important land and water features of Florida.

Statehood
Florida became the 27th state in 1845.

People & Places
Florida's population is 18,328,340. Tallahassee is the state capital. The largest city is Jacksonville.

Fun Fact
Everglades National Park is home to rare and endangered species such as the American crocodile, the Florida panther, and the West Indian manatee.

▼ The manatee is the state marine mammal of **Florida**. It averages 10 feet (3 m) in length and can weigh 1,000 pounds (450 kg).

▼ **Kennedy Space Center** on Florida's Atlantic coast has been the launch site for all U.S. human space flight missions.

Florida State Flag

Orange Blossom State Flower

Mockingbird State Bird

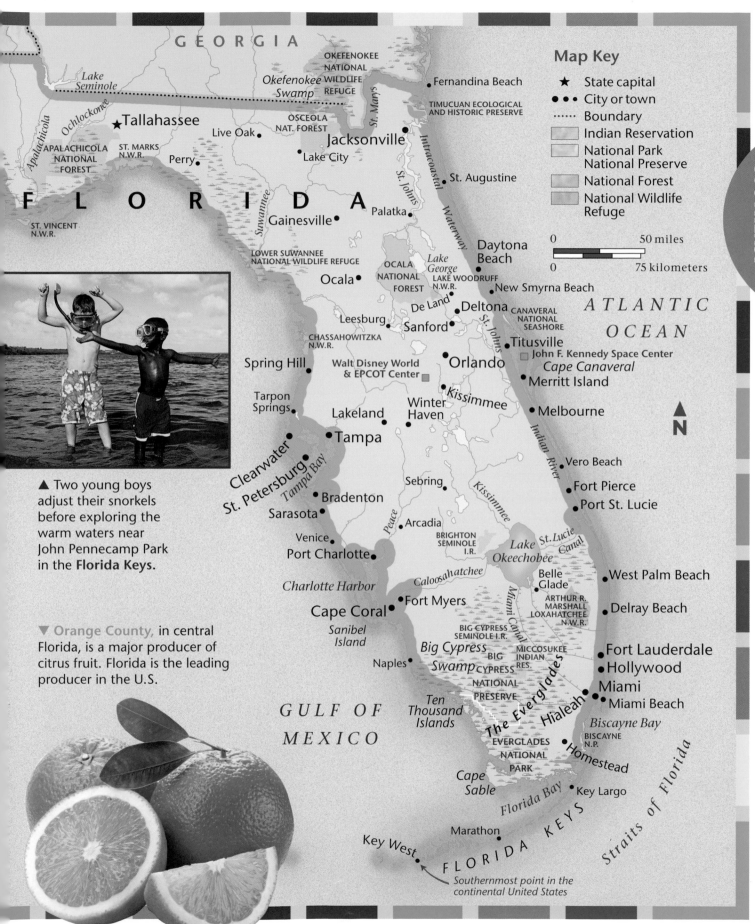

GEORGIA

Lake
Seminole

Okefenokee
Swamp

OKEEFENOKEE
NATIONAL
WILDLIFE
REFUGE

Fernandina Beach

TIMUCUAN ECOLOGICAL
AND HISTORIC PRESERVE

Ochlockonee

Apalachicola

★ **Tallahassee**

Live Oak

OSCEOLA
NAT. FOREST

ST. MARKS
N.W.R.

Perry

Jacksonville

Lake City

St. Marys

St. Johns

St. Augustine

APALACHICOLA
NATIONAL
FOREST

F L O R I D A

ST. VINCENT
N.W.R.

Gainesville

Palatka

Suwannee

LOWER SUWANNEE
NATIONAL WILDLIFE REFUGE

OCALA
NATIONAL
FOREST

Lake
George

LAKE WOODRUFF
N.W.R.

Ocala

Daytona
Beach

New Smyrna Beach

CANAVERAL
NATIONAL
SEASHORE

De Land

Deltona

St. Johns

Leesburg

Sanford

Titusville

A T L A N T I C

O C E A N

John F. Kennedy Space Center

Cape Canaveral

CHASSAHOWITZKA
N.W.R.

Spring Hill

Walt Disney World
& EPCOT Center

Orlando

Merritt Island

Intracoastal   Waterway

Tarpon
Springs

Lakeland

Winter
Haven

Kissimmee

Melbourne

Indian River

Clearwater
St. Petersburg

Tampa Bay

Tampa

Sebring

Bradenton

Sarasota

Kissimmee

Vero Beach

Fort Pierce

Port St. Lucie

Venice

Arcadia

Peace

BRIGHTON
SEMINOLE
I.R.

St. Lucie

Canal

Port Charlotte

Charlotte Harbor

Caloosahatchee

Lake
Okeechobee

Belle
Glade

West Palm Beach

Fort Myers

Cape Coral

*Sanibel
Island*

ARTHUR R.
MARSHALL
LOXAHATCHEE
N.W.R.

Delray Beach

BIG CYPRESS
SEMINOLE I.R.

Miami Canal

*Big Cypress
Swamp*

BIG
CYPRESS
NATIONAL
PRESERVE

MICCOSUKEE
INDIAN
RES.

Fort Lauderdale

Hollywood

Miami

Naples

G U L F   O F

M E X I C O

*Ten
Thousand
Islands*

The Everglades

Hialeah

Miami Beach

Biscayne Bay

EVERGLADES
NATIONAL
PARK

BISCAYNE
N.P.

Homestead

*Cape
Sable*

Key Largo

Florida Bay

F L O R I D A   K E Y S

Straits of Florida

Marathon

Key West

Southernmost point in the
continental United States

▲ Two young boys
adjust their snorkels
before exploring the
warm waters near
John Pennecamp Park
in the **Florida Keys.**

▼ **Orange County,** in central
Florida, is a major producer of
citrus fruit. Florida is the leading
producer in the U.S.

Georgia

Land & Water
The Blue Ridge Mountains, the Okefenokee Swamp, and the Savannah River are important land and water features of Georgia.

Statehood Georgia
became the 4th state in 1788.

People & Places
Georgia's population is 9,685,744. Atlanta is the state capital and the largest city.

Fun Fact The Georgia Aquarium in Atlanta is the largest aquarium in the world. It features more than 100,000 animals living in more than 8 million gallons (30.3 million liters) of water.

◀ Built for the 1996 Olympic Games, Centennial Olympic Park in **Atlanta** is the site of festivals and community events that attract an estimated 3 million visitors each year.

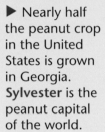

▶ Nearly half the peanut crop in the United States is grown in Georgia. **Sylvester** is the peanut capital of the world.

▼ A Great Grey Heron surveys its surroundings from its perch in a tree in the Okefenokee National Wildlife Refuge in southeastern Georgia.

Georgia State Flag

**Cherokee Rose
State Flower**

**Brown Thrasher
State Bird**

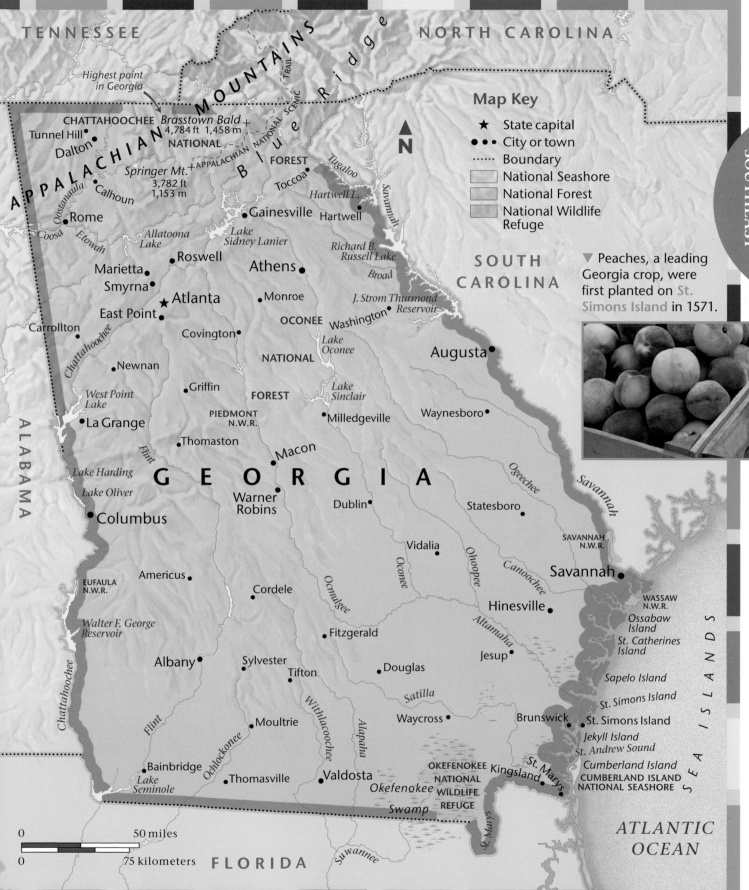

TENNESSEE

NORTH CAROLINA

Highest point in Georgia

APPALACHIAN MOUNTAINS

Blue Ridge

CHATTAHOOCHEE
Tunnel Hill
Dalton

Brasstown Bald +
4,784 ft 1,458 m

NATIONAL

APPALACHIAN NATIONAL SCENIC TRAIL

FOREST

Springer Mt.
3,782 ft
1,153 m

Oostanaula
Calhoun
Rome

Coosa

Etowah

Allatoona
Lake

Lake
Sidney Lanier

Tugaloo

Toccoa

Hartwell L.

Gainesville   Hartwell

Map Key

★ State capital
••• City or town
•••• Boundary
     National Seashore
     National Forest
     National Wildlife
     Refuge

N

Marietta
Smyrna
Roswell

Athens

Monroe

Richard B.
Russell Lake

Broad

SOUTH
CAROLINA

★ Atlanta
East Point

OCONEE

Washington

J. Strom Thurmond
Reservoir

▼ Peaches, a leading
Georgia crop, were
first planted on St.
Simons Island in 1571.

Carrollton

Covington

NATIONAL

Lake
Oconee

Augusta

Newnan

Griffin

FOREST

Lake
Sinclair

Waynesboro

Chattahoochee

West Point
Lake

La Grange

PIEDMONT
N.W.R.

Milledgeville

Thomaston

Flint

Macon

GEORGIA

Lake Harding

Lake Oliver

Warner
Robins

Dublin

Oconee

Ogeechee

Savannah

Statesboro

SAVANNAH
N.W.R.

Columbus

EUFAULA
N.W.R.

Americus

Cordele

Vidalia

Ohoopee

Canoochee

Savannah

WASSAW
N.W.R.

Walter F. George
Reservoir

Fitzgerald

Altamaha

Jesup

Hinesville

Ocmulgee

Ossabaw
Island

St. Catherines
Island

Albany

Sylvester

Tifton

Douglas

Satilla

Sapelo Island

St. Simons Island

Moultrie

Withlacoochee

Alapaha

Waycross

Brunswick

St. Simons Island

Jekyll Island

Odlockonee

Bainbridge

Thomasville

Valdosta

OKEFENOKEE
NATIONAL
WILDLIFE
REFUGE

Kingsland

St. Marys

St. Andrew Sound

Cumberland Island

CUMBERLAND ISLAND
NATIONAL SEASHORE

SEA ISLANDS

Lake
Seminole

Okefenokee
Swamp

St. Marys

ALABAMA

Flint

Chattahoochee

ATLANTIC
OCEAN

0   50 miles

0   75 kilometers

FLORIDA

Suwannee

THE
SOUTHEAST

The Southeast

▶ Shaker Village in **Pleasant Hill** preserves the culture and history of this important social movement.

Kentucky

 Land & Water Mammoth Cave, Cumberland Plateau, and the Ohio River are important land and water features of Kentucky.

 Statehood Kentucky became the 15th state in 1792.

 People & Places Kentucky's population is 4,269,245. Frankfort is the state capital. The largest city is Louisville.

Fun Fact The song "Happy Birthday to You," one of the most popular songs in the English language, was written in 1893 by two sisters living in Louisville.

◀ Abraham Lincoln, 16th President, was born near **Hodgenville**. His profile appears on the penny.

ILLINOIS

MISSOURI

Ohio

Henderson

Green

Wabash

Marion

Madisonville

Tradewater

Paducah

Cumberland

Calvert City

Hopkinsville

Princeton

Mayfield

Kentucky Lake

Little

Lake Barkley

Mayfield

LAND BETWEEN THE LAKES NAT. REC. AREA

Creek

Mississippi

Fulton

Murray

Cumberland

Tennessee

REELFOOT N.W.R.

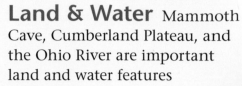

Kentucky State Flag

Goldenrod State Flower

Cardinal State Bird

▼ The setting sun turns the sky red over Cave Run Lake. The lake is a popular vacation spot because of its natural beauty.

Map Key

★ State capital
• City or town
····· Boundary
National Park
National Recreation Area
National Forest
National Wildlife Refuge

OHIO

0   50 miles
0   75 kilometers

Covington   Newport
Florence
Licking
Williamstown   Maysville   Vanceburg
North Fork   Ashland   Ohio
Cynthiana   Flemingsburg   WEST VIRGINIA
La Grange   Licking   Morehead
Kentucky   Little Sandy
B L U E G R A S S
Shelbyville   Frankfort   Paris   Mt. Sterling   Cave Run Lake   Levisa Fork   Big Sandy
Louisville   Jeffersontown   Georgetown   Lexington   Winchester   **DANIEL**
R E G I O N   Red
Brandenburg   Salt   Pleasant Hill   Kentucky   **BOONE**   North Fork   Prestonsburg   Tug Fork
Ohio   Radcliff   Bardstown   Harrodsburg   Richmond   Middle Fork   Jackson   Pikeville
Owensboro   Elizabethtown   Hodgenville   Danville   Berea   **NATIONAL**   S. Fk.   Hazard
Rough River Lake   **K E N T U C K Y**   Rolling Fork   Mount Vernon   Rockcastle   Highest point in Kentucky   **JEFFERSON**
Rough   Leitchfield   Campbellsville   Somerset   **FOREST**   London   Cumberland   **VIRGINIA**   **NATIONAL**
Nolin River Lake   Green River Lake   Corbin   Pine   Black Mt.   FOREST
Green   **MAMMOTH CAVE**   Cave City   Lake Cumberland   Cumberland   4,145 ft   **APPALACHIAN**
Pond   **NATIONAL PARK**   Glasgow   Cumberland   CUMBERLAND GAP N.H.P.   1,263 m
Bowling Green   Barren   Barren River Lake   Cumberland   Cumberland Mts.   **MOUNTAINS**
Franklin   Dale Hollow Lake   Middlesboro   Cumberland Gap

INDIANA

TENNESSEE   BIG SOUTH FORK NAT. RIVER & REC. AREA

10 9 8 7 6 5

◄ Riders in colorful jerseys astride powerful race horses charge out of the starting gate during a race in **Kentucky**. The state is a major producer of thoroughbred race horses.

The Southeast

▲ Musicians practice on a park bench in **New Orleans** as they wait for one of the city's Mardi Gras parades to begin.

Louisiana

Land & Water Driskill Mountain, Lake Pontchartrain, and the Mississippi River are important land and water features of Louisiana.

Statehood Louisiana became the 18th state in 1812.

People & Places Louisiana's population is 4,410,796. Baton Rouge is the state capital and the largest city.

Fun Fact The Louisiana State Capitol building in Baton Rouge is the tallest of all the state capitols. It is a limestone skyscraper that stands 450 feet (137 m) tall and has 34 stories!

▲ The *Mississippi Queen*, a paddle wheel boat, churns up the water as it steams along the Mississippi River between **Baton Rouge** and New Orleans.

Louisiana State Flag

UNION, JUSTICE & CONFIDENCE

Magnolia State Flower

Brown Pelican State Bird

◀ Louisiana produces almost half the shrimp caught in the U.S. Most of it comes from the Barataria-Terrebonne estuary of the Mississippi River.

Map labels: Springhill, KISATCHIE NATIONAL FOREST, Caddo Lake, Red, Bossier City, Minden, Shreveport, Lake Bistineau, Mansfield, Red, Toledo Bend Reservoir, Natchitoches, Many, Leesville, TEXAS, De Ridder, Sabine, De Quincy, Lake Charles, Sulphur, Intracoastal, Calcasieu Lake, CAMERON PRAIRIE N.W.R., Sabine Lake, SABINE NAT. WILDLIFE REFUGE

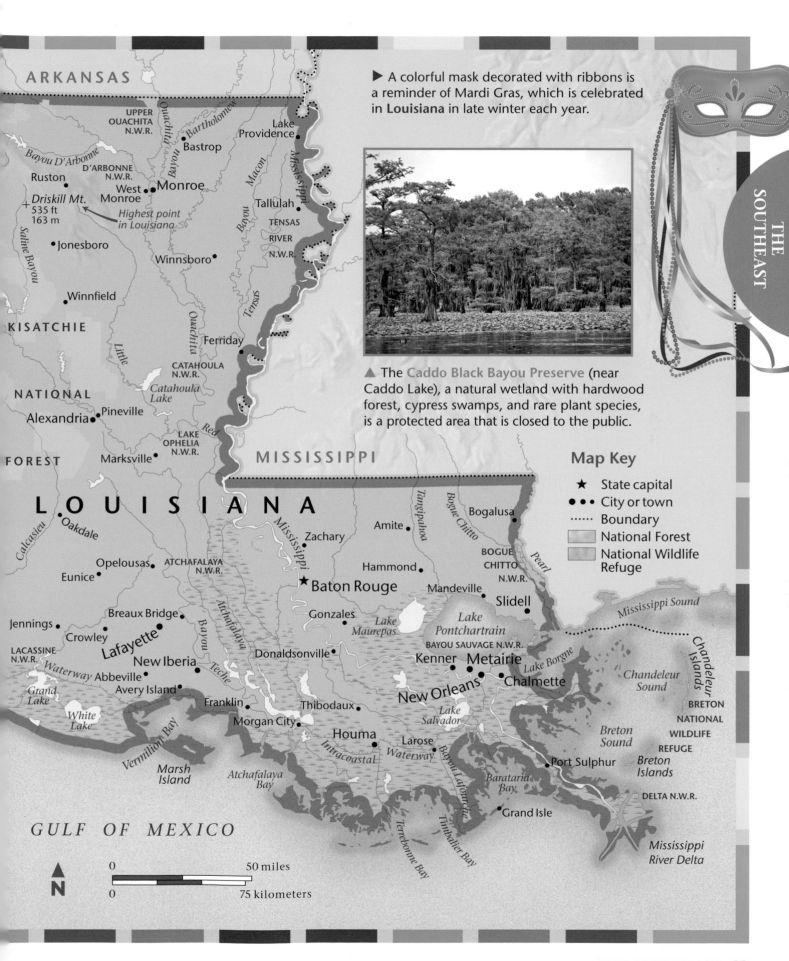

ARKANSAS

UPPER
OUACHITA
N.W.R.

Bayou D'Arbonne

D'ARBONNE
N.W.R.

Ruston
West
Monroe • Monroe

Driskill Mt.
535 ft
163 m
*Highest point
in Louisiana*

• Jonesboro

Lake
Providence
• Bastrop

Tallulah

TENSAS
RIVER
N.W.R.

Winnsboro

KISATCHIE

Ferriday

CATAHOULA
N.W.R.

Catahoula
Lake

NATIONAL

Alexandria • Pineville

LAKE
OPHELIA
N.W.R.

FOREST   Marksville

► A colorful mask decorated with ribbons is
a reminder of Mardi Gras, which is celebrated
in **Louisiana** in late winter each year.

▲ The Caddo Black Bayou Preserve (near
Caddo Lake), a natural wetland with hardwood
forest, cypress swamps, and rare plant species,
is a protected area that is closed to the public.

MISSISSIPPI

THE
SOUTHEAST

Map Key

★ State capital
••• City or town
····· Boundary
▭ National Forest
▭ National Wildlife
Refuge

L O U I S I A N A

Oakdale

Calcasieu

Opelousas

ATCHAFALAYA
N.W.R.

Eunice

Zachary

Amite

Bogalusa

BOGUE
CHITTO
N.W.R.

Hammond

★ Baton Rouge

Mandeville

Slidell

Jennings
Crowley

Breaux Bridge

Lafayette

LACASSINE
N.W.R.

Waterway   Abbeville

Grand
Lake

White
Lake

New Iberia

Avery Island

Franklin

Morgan City

Marsh
Island

Vermilion Bay

Atchafalaya
Bay

G U L F   O F   M E X I C O

Donaldsonville

Gonzales

Lake
Maurepas

Lake
Pontchartrain

BAYOU SAUVAGE N.W.R.

Kenner Metairie

New Orleans   Chalmette

Lake
Salvador

Houma

Larose

Intracoastal
Waterway

Thibodaux

Lake Borgne

Mississippi Sound

Chandeleur
Sound

BRETON

NATIONAL

WILDLIFE

REFUGE

Breton
Sound

Breton
Islands

Chandeleur Islands

Barataria
Bay

Port Sulphur

Grand Isle

DELTA N.W.R.

Terrebonne Bay

Timbalier Bay

Mississippi
River Delta

N

0   50 miles
0   75 kilometers

The Southeast

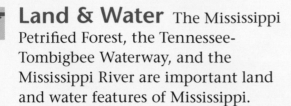

Mississippi

Land & Water The Mississippi Petrified Forest, the Tennessee-Tombigbee Waterway, and the Mississippi River are important land and water features of Mississippi.

Statehood Mississippi became the 20th state in 1817.

People & Places Mississippi's population is 2,938,618. Jackson is the state capital and the largest city.

Fun Fact Jim Henson, creator of Kermit the Frog, Miss Piggy, Big Bird, and other famous Muppets, was born in Greenville.

▲ Mississippi is the leading producer of catfish in the U.S. A part of the **Mississippi River** valley known as the Delta is the main producing area.

▲ Two bridges stretch across the Mississippi River in the town of **Vicksburg.** The river is home to more than 400 species of wildlife.

▼ Children play in a tidal pool on a **Biloxi** beach as the sun sets. Barrier islands separate the city from the Gulf of Mexico.

Mississippi State Flag

Mockingbird State Bird

Magnolia State Flower

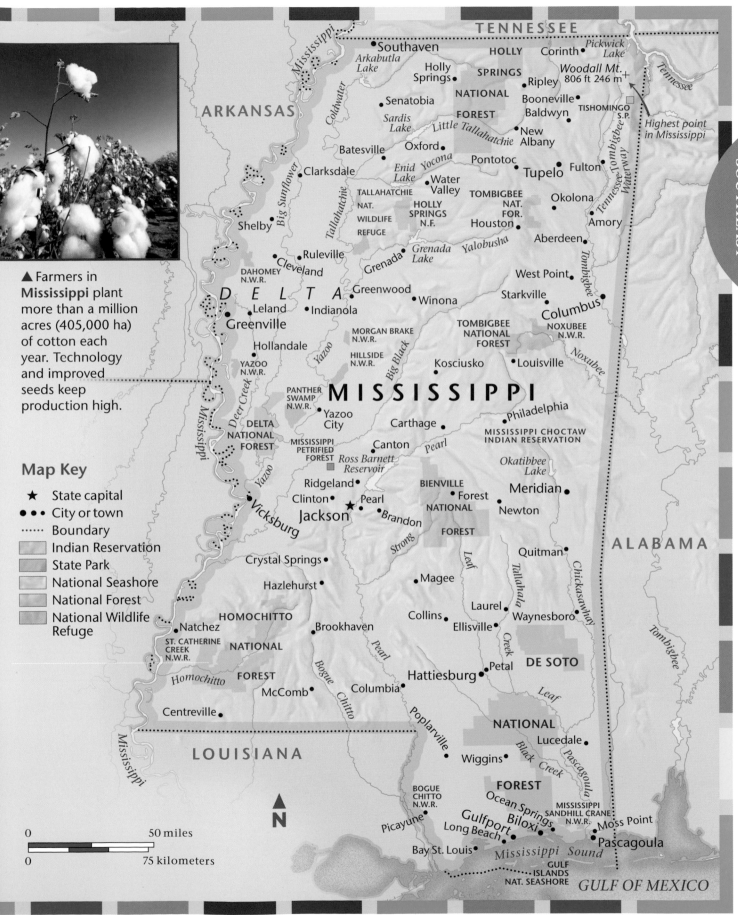

ARKANSAS

Mississippi

Southaven
Arkabutla Lake
Coldwater
Senatobia
Sardis Lake
Batesville
Clarksdale
Enid Lake
Yocona
Tallahatchie
Shelby
Big Sunflower
Ruleville
Cleveland
DAHOMEY N.W.R.

D E L T A
Leland
Indianola
Greenville
Hollandale
YAZOO N.W.R.
Deer Creek
Mississippi

HOLLY
SPRINGS
NATIONAL
FOREST
Little Tallahatchie
Oxford
Water Valley
TALLAHATCHIE NAT. WILDLIFE REFUGE
HOLLY SPRINGS N.F.
Grenada
Grenada Lake
Yalobusha
Greenwood
Winona
Yazoo
MORGAN BRAKE N.W.R.
HILLSIDE N.W.R.
Big Black

Corinth
Pickwick Lake
Holly Springs
Ripley
Booneville
Baldwyn
New Albany
Pontotoc
Tupelo
Fulton
TOMBIGBEE NAT. FOR.
Houston
Okolona
Aberdeen
West Point
Starkville
Columbus
TOMBIGBEE NATIONAL FOREST
NOXUBEE N.W.R.
Noxubee
Kosciusko
Louisville

Woodall Mt.
806 ft 246 m
TISHOMINGO S.P.
Tennessee
Tennessee-Tombigbee Waterway

Highest point in Mississippi

Tombigbee

PANTHER SWAMP N.W.R.
Yazoo City
MISSISSIPPI PETRIFIED FOREST
DELTA NATIONAL FOREST
Ridgeland
Clinton
Vicksburg
Jackson
Yazoo
Canton
Carthage
Pearl
Ross Barnett Reservoir
Pearl
Brandon
Strong
Crystal Springs
Hazlehurst

MISSISSIPPI

Philadelphia
MISSISSIPPI CHOCTAW INDIAN RESERVATION
Okatibbee Lake
BIENVILLE
Forest
NATIONAL
FOREST
Newton
Meridian
Quitman
Leaf
Magee
Tallahala
Collins
Laurel
Waynesboro
Ellisville
Chickasawhay
Tombigbee
ALABAMA

HOMOCHITTO
Natchez
ST. CATHERINE CREEK N.W.R.
NATIONAL
Homochitto
FOREST
McComb
Bogue Chitto
Brookhaven
Columbia
Pearl
Centreville

Hattiesburg
Petal
DE SOTO
Leaf
NATIONAL
Lucedale
Poplarville
Black Creek
Pascagoula
Wiggins
FOREST
BOGUE CHITTO N.W.R.
Ocean Springs
MISSISSIPPI SANDHILL CRANE N.W.R.
Picayune
Gulfport
Biloxi
Moss Point
Long Beach
Pascagoula
Bay St. Louis
Mississippi Sound
GULF ISLANDS NAT. SEASHORE

Mississippi
LOUISIANA

GULF OF MEXICO

Map Key

★ State capital
••• City or town
····· Boundary
　 Indian Reservation
　 State Park
　 National Seashore
　 National Forest
　 National Wildlife Refuge

▲ Farmers in **Mississippi** plant more than a million acres (405,000 ha) of cotton each year. Technology and improved seeds keep production high.

N

| 0 | | 50 miles |
| 0 | | 75 kilometers |

North Carolina

Land & Water Mount Mitchell, the Outer Banks, and the Cape Fear River are important land and water features of North Carolina.

Statehood North Carolina became the 12th state in 1789.

People & Places North Carolina's population is 9,222,414. Raleigh is the state capital. The largest city is Charlotte.

Fun Fact The University of North Carolina, the first public university in the U. S., opened its doors in 1795 with 2 professors and 41 students.

0 — 50 miles
0 — 75 kilometers

TENNESSEE

Highest point in North Carolina and east of the Mississippi

Boone

French Broad

APPALACHIAN

NATIONAL SCENIC TRAIL

PISGAH

Mt. Mitchell 6,684 ft 2,037 m

Lenoir

Catawba

GREAT SMOKY MOUNTAINS NATIONAL PARK

Great Smoky Mts.

NATIONAL

Asheville

Morganton

Hickory

Fontana L.

CHEROKEE I.R.

FOREST

Hendersonville

Shelby

Hiwassee L.

NANTAHALA

NATIONAL

Franklin

Broad

FOREST

APPALACHIAN

Chattooga

GEORGIA

SOUTH

North Carolina State Flag

Cardinal
State Bird

Flowering Dogwood
State Flower

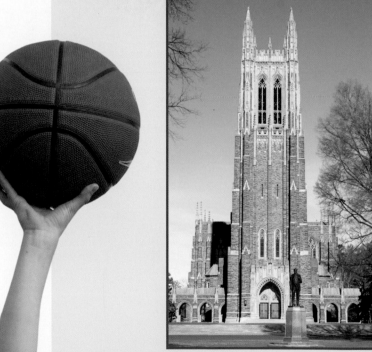

▲ The chapel tower is a landmark on the campus of Duke University in **Durham.**

◄ Basketball is a popular sport among all ages in **North Carolina,** whether on the court or in the backyard.

VIRGINIA

GREAT DISMAL SWAMP N.W.R.
Great Dismal Swamp
MACKAY ISLAND N.W.R.

Mt. Airy
Eden
Dan
New
Roanoke Rapids
Lake Gaston
Roanoke
Chowan
Elizabeth City
Kitty Hawk

Reidsville
John H. Kerr Reservoir
Roxboro
Henderson
Edenton
Roanoke Island

Greensboro
Haw
Burlington
Falls L.
Rocky Mount
Williamston
Albemarle Sound
ALLIGATOR RIVER N.W.R.
Hatteras Island

Winston-Salem
High Point
Chapel Hill
Durham
Raleigh
POCOSIN LAKES N.W.R.

Yadkin
Statesville
Lexington
Salisbury
B. Everett Jordan Lake
Cary
Garner
Wilson
Tar
Washington
MATTAMUSKEET N.W.R.
CAPE HATTERAS NATIONAL SEASHORE

Lake Norman
Asheboro
Sanford
Goldsboro
SWANQUARTER N.W.R.

N O R T H   C A R O L I N A
Deep
Pamlico Sound
Outer Banks

Kannapolis
Concord
UWHARRIE NATIONAL FOREST
Dunn
Kinston
New Bern
CEDAR ISLAND N.W.R.
Ocracoke Island
Cape Hatteras

Gastonia
Albemarle
Pinehurst
Neuse
CROATAN NAT. FOREST
Havelock
Neuse R.
CAPE LOOKOUT NATIONAL SEASHORE
Raleigh Bay

Charlotte
PEE DEE N.W.R.
Fayetteville
Clinton
Jacksonville
Morehead City
ATLANTIC OCEAN

Monroe
Laurinburg
Lumber
Lumberton
South
Cape Fear

CAROLINA
Pee Dee
Whiteville
Lake Waccamaw
Wilmington
Wrightsville Beach
Onslow Bay
Cape Lookout

Green Swamp
Southport
Map Key

Intracoastal Waterway
Long Bay
Cape Fear

N

THE SOUTHEAST

Map Key

★ State capital
••• City or town
⋯⋯ Boundary
Indian Reservation
National Park
National Seashore
National Forest
National Wildlife Refuge

◀ Cape Lookout Lighthouse on the **Outer Banks** has warned ships of dangerous sandbars since it began operation in 1812.

▶ Orville and Wilbur Wright, from Dayton, Ohio, made the first successful airplane flight near Kitty Hawk on North Carolina's Outer Banks.

The Southeast

South Carolina

 Land & Water The Blue Ridge Mountains, Lake Marion, and the Cooper River are important land and water features of South Carolina.

 Statehood South Carolina became the 8th state in 1788.

 People & Places South Carolina's population is 4,479,800. Columbia is the state capital and the largest city.

? **Fun Fact** Sweetgrass baskets have been made in the coastal lowland region for more than 300 years. They were originally used in the planting and processing of rice.

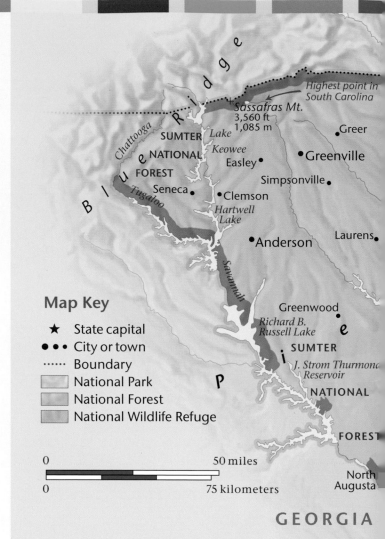

Map Key

★ State capital
●●● City or town
...... Boundary
National Park
National Forest
National Wildlife Refuge

0   50 miles
0   75 kilometers

GEORGIA

Highest point in South Carolina
Sassafras Mt.
3,560 ft
1,085 m

Greer
Greenville
Easley
Simpsonville
Seneca
Clemson
Hartwell Lake
Anderson
Laurens
Greenwood
Richard B. Russell Lake
SUMTER
J. Strom Thurmond Reservoir
NATIONAL
FOREST
North Augusta

SUMTER
Lake
NATIONAL
FOREST
Keowee
Chattooga
Tugaloo
Savannah

▼ Large container ships carrying valuable manufactured goods link South Carolina to the global economy. Charleston is the state's largest port.

South Carolina State Flag

Yellow Jessamine
State Flower

Carolina Wren
State Bird

NORTH CAROLINA

Gaffney
Spartanburg
York
Rock Hill
Union
Chester
Lancaster
Cheraw
SUMTER
NATIONAL
FOREST
Newberry
Winnsboro
CAROLINA
SANDHILLS
N.W.R.
Hartsville
Dillon
Darlington
Florence
Marion
Lake Murray
Irmo
SOUTH
West Columbia
Columbia
Loris
Cayce
Sumter
Conway
Myrtle Beach
CONGAREE
NATIONAL PARK
Lake City
Edgefield
CAROLINA
Garden City
Aiken
Orangeburg
Georgetown
Williston
Lake Marion
North Island
Bamberg
Lake Moultrie
FRANCIS MARION NATIONAL FOREST
ATLANTIC
Allendale
Moncks Corner
Cape Island
OCEAN
Summerville
CAPE ROMAIN N.W.R.
Walterboro
Hanahan
North Charleston
Charleston
Mount Pleasant
Edisto Island
Beaufort
St. Helena Sound
St. Helena Island
Parris Island
Port Royal Sound
SEA ISLANDS
SAVANNAH
NATIONAL
WILDLIFE
REFUGE
Hilton Head Island
Hilton Head Island
Daufuskie Island

Broad
Wylie Lake
Catawba
Wateree Lake
Wateree
Great Pee Dee
Saluda
Congaree
Lynches
Little Pee Dee
Great Pee Dee
Waccamaw
Intracoastal Waterway
Long Bay
Black
N. Fork Edisto
S. Fork Edisto
Santee
Edisto
Cooper
Savannah
Coosawhatchie
Combahee

Piedmont

Coastal Plain

▲ Alligators are native to swamps and streams of South Carolina. They are especially common in the coastal area known as the **Lowcountry**.

▼ Hard-packed sands on a **Hilton Head Island** beach are perfect for a family bicycle outing.

Tennessee

 Land & Water The Appalachian Mountains, Reelfoot Lake, and the Tennessee River are important land and water features of Tennessee.

 Statehood Tennessee became the 16th state in 1796.

 People & Places Tennessee's population is 6,214,888. Nashville is the state capital. The largest city is Memphis.

Fun Fact Graceland, Elvis Presley's colonial-style 23-room mansion and estate in Memphis, was declared a National Historic Landmark in 2006. It is the second most visited house in the country.

MISSOURI

Mississippi

Kentucky Lake
LAND BETWEEN
THE LAKES
NATIONAL REC. AREA

Lake

REELFOOT
N.W.R.
Reelfoot L.
Obion

Union City
Martin
Dyersburg

Paris
TENNESSEE

ARKANSAS

CHICKASAW
N.W.R.

Brownsville
Jackson

NATIONAL

WILDLIFE

REFUGE

LOWER HATCHIE
N.W.R.
HATCHIE
N.W.R.

Mississippi

Millington
Bartlett
Germantown
Collierville

Memphis

Hatchie

Savannah

Pickwick
Lake

Tennessee

Tennessee

MISSISSIPPI

Tennessee State Flag

Iris
State Flower

Mockingbird
State Bird

► **Memphis** is famous for its barbecue, especially baby back ribs that are cooked so long that the meat falls from the bones.

▼ Norris Dam, on a tributary of the **Tennessee River**, was completed in 1936. It was constructed to generate electricity.

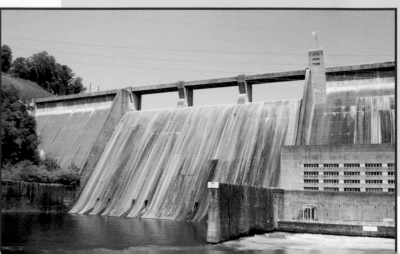

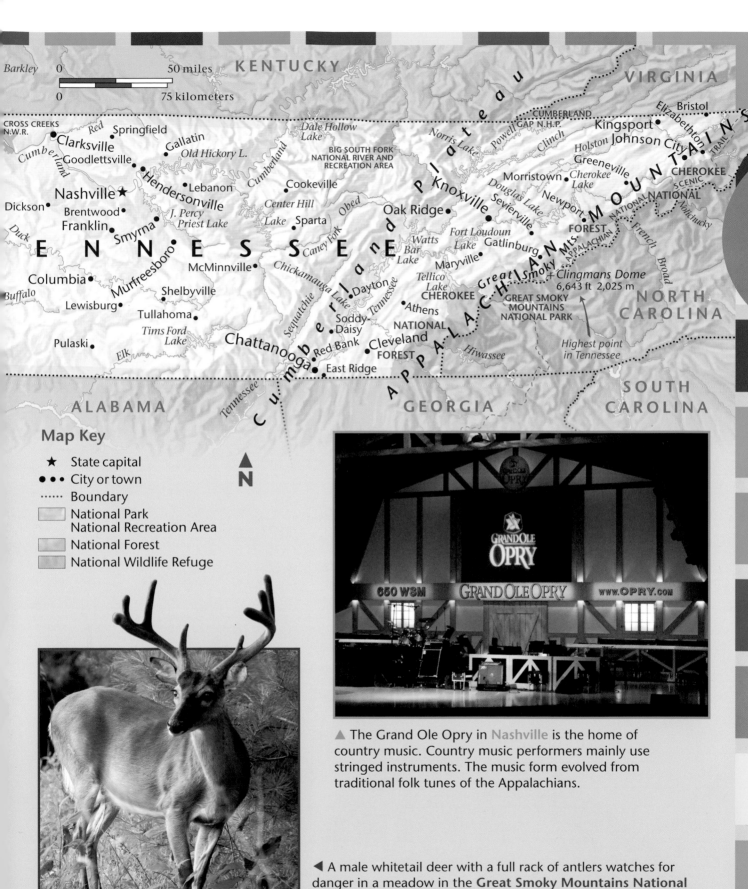

KENTUCKY

VIRGINIA

Barkley 0   50 miles

0   75 kilometers

Bristol

CROSS CREEKS N.W.R.

Red

Springfield

Clarksville

Goodlettsville

Dale Hollow Lake

Norris Lake

CUMBERLAND GAP N.H.P.

Powell

Clinch

Kingsport

Elizabethton

Johnson City

Cumberland

Gallatin

Old Hickory L.

BIG SOUTH FORK NATIONAL RIVER AND RECREATION AREA

Holston

Greeneville

CHEROKEE

Nashville ★

Hendersonville

Lebanon

Cookeville

Cumberland

Knoxville

Morristown

Cherokee Lake

Newport

NATIONAL

SCENIC

Dickson

Center Hill Lake

Obed

Oak Ridge

Douglas Lake

Sevierville

FOREST

Nolichucky

Brentwood

T E N N E S S E E

Franklin

J. Percy Priest Lake

Sparta

Caney Fork

Watts Bar Lake

Fort Loudoun Lake

Gatlinburg

APPALACHIAN

French Broad

Smyrna

M O U N T A I N S

Duck

Columbia

Murfreesboro

McMinnville

Chickamauga Lake

Dayton

Tellico Lake

Maryville

Smoky Mts.

Great Smoky Mts.

Clingmans Dome 6,643 ft 2,025 m

NORTH CAROLINA

Buffalo

Lewisburg

Shelbyville

CHEROKEE

Highest point in Tennessee

Pulaski

Tullahoma

Tims Ford Lake

Sequatchie

Soddy-Daisy

Tennessee

Athens

NATIONAL

GREAT SMOKY MOUNTAINS NATIONAL PARK

Elk

Chattanooga

Red Bank

Cleveland

FOREST

Hiwassee

East Ridge

ALABAMA

Tennessee

GEORGIA

SOUTH CAROLINA

Map Key

★   State capital

•••   City or town

·····   Boundary

   National Park National Recreation Area

   National Forest

   National Wildlife Refuge

N

GRAND OLE OPRY

650 WSM   GRAND OLE OPRY   www.OPRY.com

▲ The Grand Ole Opry in Nashville is the home of country music. Country music performers mainly use stringed instruments. The music form evolved from traditional folk tunes of the Appalachians.

◄ A male whitetail deer with a full rack of antlers watches for danger in a meadow in the **Great Smoky Mountains National Park.** The park is a popular vacation destination.

The Southeast

Virginia

Land & Water
The Appalachian Mountains, Luray Caverns, and the James River are important land and water features of Virginia.

Statehood
Virginia became the 10th state in 1788.

People & Places
Virginia's population is 7,769,089. Richmond is the state capital. The largest city is Virginia Beach.

Fun Fact
Eight U.S. Presidents—Washington, Jefferson, Madison, Monroe, Harrison, Tyler, Taylor, and Wilson—were born in Virginia, more than any other state.

Virginia State Flag

Flowering Dogwood State Flower

Cardinal State Bird

▲ An old barn, bales of hay, and trees in autumn foliage are a common sight in the **Appalachian Mountains** of Virginia.

0   50 miles
0   75 kilometers

N

KENTUCKY

TENNESSEE

A l l e g h

JEFFERSON

Clinch

Bluefield

Wytheville

NAT

CUMBERLAND GAP N.H.P.

Powell

Big Stone Gap

Clinch Mtn.

North Fork

Marion

Bristol

MOUNT ROGERS N.R.A.

Mt. Rogers
5,729 ft
1,746 m

Holston

S. Fork

APPALA

▼ A fife and drum band dressed in British colors marches down a street in colonial **Williamsburg**, an early capital of Virginia.

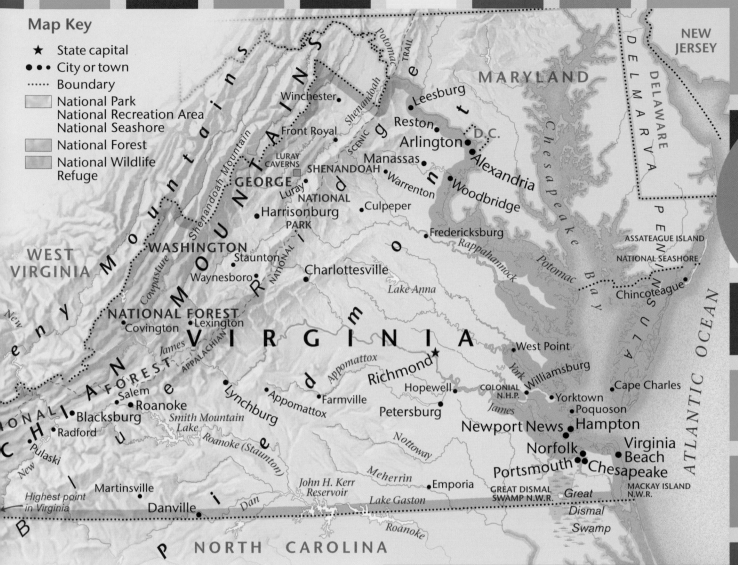

Map Key

★ State capital
●●● City or town
⋯⋯ Boundary
▢ National Park
National Recreation Area
National Seashore
▢ National Forest
▢ National Wildlife Refuge

NEW JERSEY

DELAWARE

DELMARVA PENINSULA

MARYLAND

WEST VIRGINIA

Winchester
Leesburg
Front Royal
Reston
D.C.
Arlington
Manassas
Alexandria
LURAY CAVERNS
SHENANDOAH
Warrenton
Woodbridge
GEORGE
Luray
NATIONAL
Harrisonburg
PARK
Culpeper
WASHINGTON
Fredericksburg
Staunton
Rappahannock
Waynesboro
Charlottesville
Lake Anna
Chincoteague
ASSATEAGUE ISLAND
NATIONAL SEASHORE
Potomac Bay
Chesapeake Bay

Compasture
NATIONAL FOREST
Covington Lexington
James
VIRGINIA
West Point
Richmond
Williamsburg
Appomattox
Cape Charles
Salem
Appomattox
Farmville
Hopewell
COLONIAL N.H.P.
Yorktown
Roanoke
Petersburg
James
Poquoson
Blacksburg
Smith Mountain Lake
Newport News
Hampton
Radford
Roanoke (Staunton)
Nottoway
Norfolk
Virginia Beach
Pulaski
Meherrin
Portsmouth
Chesapeake
New
Martinsville
John H. Kerr Reservoir
Emporia
GREAT DISMAL SWAMP N.W.R.
Great Dismal Swamp
MACKAY ISLAND N.W.R.

Highest point in Virginia
Danville
Dan
Lake Gaston
Roanoke

ATLANTIC OCEAN

NORTH CAROLINA

► Winding under the Appalachian Mountains, **Luray Caverns** formed as water dissolved rocks and the minerals dripped down to form stalactites and stalagmites.

◄ The sharp eyes of a Great Blue Heron watch the water of a river near Richmond for a dinner of fish or frogs.

West Virginia

Land & Water The Allegheny Mountains, Elk River, and the New River are important land and water features of West Virginia.

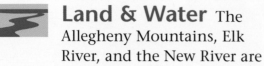

Statehood West Virginia became the 35th state in 1863.

People & Places West Virginia's population is 1,814,468. Charleston is the state capital and the largest city.

Fun Fact One of the oldest and largest Indian burial grounds is located in Moundsville. It is more than 2,000 years old and 69 feet (21 m) high.

▲ West Virginia's rivers offer some of the best whitewater rafting in the eastern U.S. The **Gauley River** is called the Beast of the East.

◄ A coal miner's helmet recalls the history of mining in **West Virginia**. The state produced 13 percent of U.S. coal in 2006.

▼ Trees turn red in the **Dolly Sods Wilderness** in the Monongahela National Forest. The area is named for an early settler family.

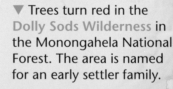

West Virginia State Flag

Rhododendron State Flower

Cardinal State Bird

Point Pleasant

Kanawha

Ohio

Hurricane

Huntington

Big Sandy

Guyandotte

Tug Fork

Logan

Williamson

KENTUCKY

A

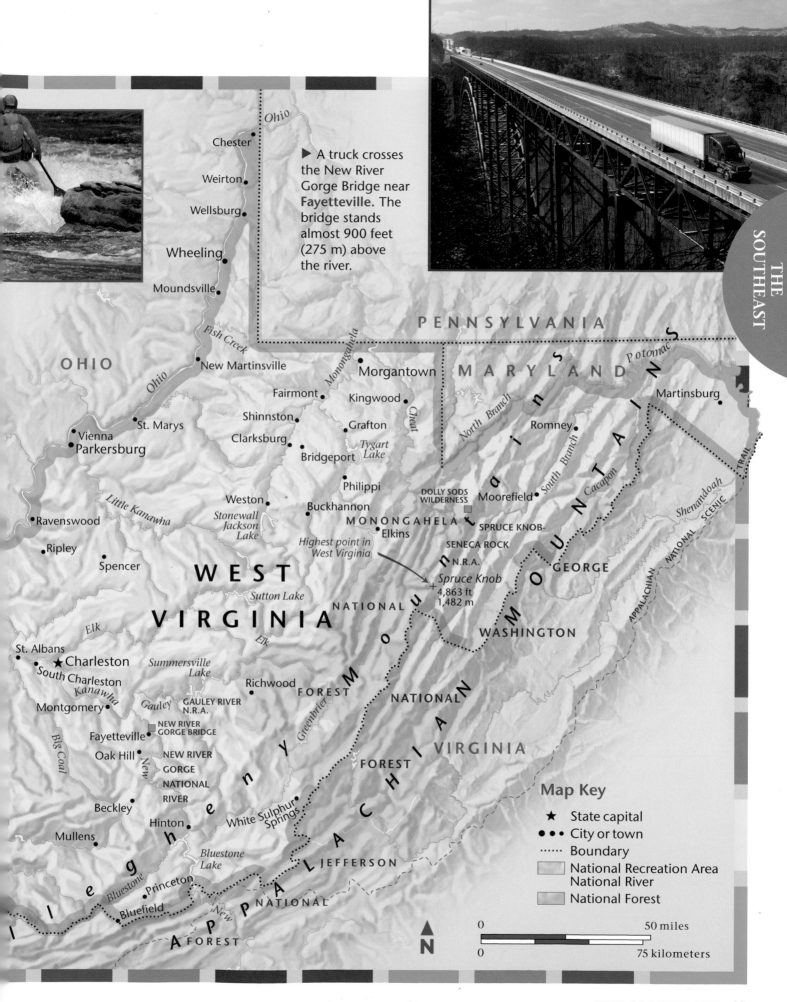

► A truck crosses the New River Gorge Bridge near **Fayetteville**. The bridge stands almost 900 feet (275 m) above the river.

PENNSYLVANIA

OHIO

MARYLAND

Ohio

Chester

Weirton

Wellsburg

Wheeling

Moundsville

Fish Creek

New Martinsville

Ohio

Morgantown

Monongahela

Fairmont

Kingwood

Potomac

Martinsburg

North Branch

Romney

St. Marys

Shinnston

Grafton

Cheat

South Branch

Cacapon

Vienna
Parkersburg

Clarksburg

Bridgeport

Tygart Lake

Little Kanawha

Ravenswood

Weston

Philippi

Buckhannon

DOLLY SODS
WILDERNESS

Moorefield

Shenandoah

SCENIC

TRAIL

Ripley

*Stonewall
Jackson
Lake*

M O N O N G A H E L A

Elkins

SPRUCE KNOB-
SENECA ROCK

GEORGE

Spencer

*Highest point in
West Virginia*

N.R.A.

APPALACHIAN

NATIONAL

W E S T

Sutton Lake

NATIONAL

Spruce Knob
4,863 ft
1,482 m

V I R G I N I A

Elk

Elk

WASHINGTON

St. Albans

★ Charleston

*Summersville
Lake*

Richwood

FOREST

NATIONAL

South Charleston

Kanawha

Montgomery

Gauley

GAULEY RIVER
N.R.A.

VIRGINIA

Fayetteville

NEW RIVER
GORGE BRIDGE

FOREST

Oak Hill

New

NEW RIVER
GORGE
NATIONAL
RIVER

Beckley

Hinton

White Sulphur
Springs

JEFFERSON

Mullens

*Bluestone
Lake*

Big Coal

Map Key

★ State capital

••• City or town

•••• Boundary

National Recreation Area
National River

National Forest

Bluestone

Princeton

Bluefield

NATIONAL

New

FOREST

0   50 miles

0   75 kilometers

N

The Midwest

The Midwest is a region of glacier-carved lakes, mighty rivers, and rolling prairies. The Great Lakes are among the largest freshwater lakes in the world. The Mississippi River and its tributaries—the Missouri and the Ohio Rivers—drain America's heartland. The region's lowlands and plains support some of the most productive agriculture in the world. Industries such as food processing, steel, and automobile production supported the growth of cities such as Pittsburgh, Chicago, and St. Louis, but they are being replaced by businesses based on technology and information.

The setting sun turns this Kansas prairie a golden red. The Midwest is a major grain-producing region. Dairy cows are also an important part of the region's economy, supplying much of the country's milk, cheese, and butter.

Illinois

Land & Water

The Shawnee National Forest, the Illinois River, and Lake Michigan are important land and water features of Illinois.

Statehood Illinois

became the 21st state in 1818.

People & Places

Illinois's population is 12,901,563. Springfield is the state capital. The largest city is Chicago.

Fun Fact The Chicago

River is dyed green on St. Patrick's Day to honor the city's large Irish population. The formula for the green dye is a closely kept secret.

◄ Children ride bicycles along a sidewalk in Pilsen, on **Chicago**'s lower west side. A street mural provides a clue to the neighborhood's immigrant population.

▲ Pig races are a fun-filled highlight of the annual **Illinois** State Fair in Springfield.

Illinois State Flag

**Violet
State Flower**

**Cardinal
State Bird**

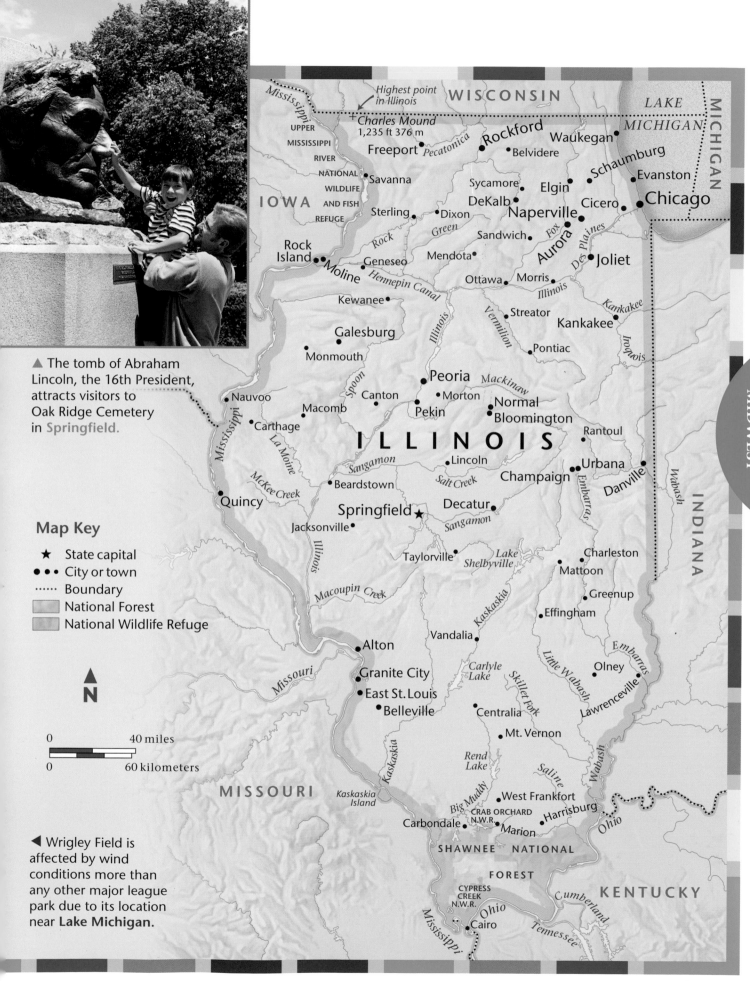

The tomb of Abraham Lincoln, the 16th President, attracts visitors to Oak Ridge Cemetery in **Springfield**.

Map Key

★ State capital
• • • City or town
······ Boundary
National Forest
National Wildlife Refuge

N

0   40 miles
0   60 kilometers

◄ Wrigley Field is affected by wind conditions more than any other major league park due to its location near **Lake Michigan**.

Highest point in Illinois
+ Charles Mound 1,235 ft 376 m

WISCONSIN

LAKE MICHIGAN

MICHIGAN

Mississippi

UPPER MISSISSIPPI RIVER NATIONAL WILDLIFE AND FISH REFUGE

IOWA

Freeport   *Pecatonica*   Rockford   Waukegan
Savanna   Belvidere   Schaumburg
              Sycamore   Elgin   Evanston
Sterling   DeKalb   Naperville Cicero Chicago
         Dixon   *Green*   *Fox*
Rock Island   Sandwich   Aurora *Des Plaines* Joliet
Moline   Geneseo   Mendota   Morris
Rock   *Hennepin Canal*   Ottawa   *Illinois*
         Kewanee   *Kankakee*
                           Illinois   Streator   Kankakee
Galesburg   *Vermilion*   Pontiac   *Iroquois*
   Monmouth
                    Spoon   Peoria   *Mackinaw*
              Canton   Morton   Normal
   Macomb   Pekin   Bloomington
Nauvoo   Rantoul
Mississippi   Carthage   **ILLINOIS**
         La Moine   Lincoln   Urbana
                  Sangamon   Champaign   Danville   *Wabash*
   McKee Creek   *Salt Creek*
Quincy   Beardstown   INDIANA
         Springfield ★   Decatur
Jacksonville   *Sangamon*
                                    Charleston
         Taylorville   *Lake Shelbyville*   Mattoon
   Illinois   Greenup
              Macoupin Creek   Effingham   *Embarras*
                                 Vandalia
Alton   Olney
                     Carlyle Lake   *Skillet Fork*   *Little Wabash*
Granite City   Lawrenceville
East St. Louis   *Kaskaskia*
   Belleville   Centralia
                        Mt. Vernon
Missouri   *Embarras*
         Kaskaskia   *Rend Lake*   *Saline*   *Wabash*
MISSOURI   West Frankfort
   Kaskaskia Island   *Big Muddy*   Harrisburg
                  CRAB ORCHARD N.W.R.   *Ohio*
         Carbondale   Marion
              SHAWNEE NATIONAL
                  FOREST   KENTUCKY
         CYPRESS CREEK N.W.R.   *Cumberland*
Mississippi   Cairo   *Ohio*
                           Tennessee

The Midwest

Indiana

Land & Water The Hoosier National Forest, Lake Michigan, and the Wabash River are important land and water features of Indiana.

Statehood Indiana became the 19th state in 1816.

People & Places Indiana's population is 6,376,792. Indianapolis is the state capital and the largest city.

Fun Fact The intersection of U.S. Highway 40 and U.S. Highway 41 in Terre Haute, at Wabash Avenue and Seventh Street, is called the "Crossroads of America."

▲ The Indianapolis Motor Speedway is the largest sports stadium in the world. It seats 250,000 and hosts the famous Indy 500.

▶ The Hoosiers of Indiana University, located in **Bloomington**, are a part of the powerful Big Ten Conference. Sports are a big tradition and favorite pastime in Indiana.

Indiana State Flag

Peony
State Flower

Cardinal
State Bird

Map Key

★ State capital
●●● City or town
······ Boundary
State Park
National Lakeshore
National Forest
National Wildlife Refuge

0 ——— 100 miles
0 ——— 150 kilometers

N

▼ A boy gathers sweet corn on the family farm near **Centerville.** Corn is an important food for both people and livestock.

LAKE MICHIGAN

MICHIGAN

East Chicago
Hammond
Michigan City
INDIANA DUNES NAT. LAKESHORE
St. Joseph
Elkhart
Pigeon
Angola
South Bend
Mishawaka
Goshen
Gary
Portage
Merrillville
Valparaiso
Crown Point
Lake Wawasee
Auburn
Cedar Creek
Plymouth
Warsaw
St. Joseph
Kankakee
Tippecanoe
Fort Wayne
Maumee
Rensselaer
Eel
Huntington
Huntington Lake
St. Marys
Iroquois
Lake Shafer
Logansport
Wabash
Peru
Salamonie Lake
Wabash
Lake Freeman
Wabash
Mississinewa Lake
Salamonie

INDIANA

Kokomo
Marion
Salamonie
Lafayette
Wildcat Creek
Mississinewa
Frankfort
Muncie
Highest point in Indiana
White
Crawfordsville
Lebanon
Noblesville
Anderson
1,257 ft 383 m
Wabash
Sugar Creek
Carmel
Sugar Creek
New Castle
Richmond
Big Raccoon Creek
Lawrence
Greenfield
Centerville
Cecil M. Harden Lake
Indianapolis ★
Beech Grove
Connersville
Plainfield
Big Blue
Mill Creek
Greenwood
Shelbyville
Brookville Lake
Cagles Mill Lake
White
Franklin
Flatrock
Terre Haute
Martinsville
Greensburg
Whitewater
Great Miami
Eel
Lake Lemon
Columbus
Bloomington
BROWN COUNTY STATE PARK
Sand Creek
Lawrenceburg
Monroe Lake
Seymour
Ohio
Salt Cr.
HOOSIER
MUSCATATUCK N.W.R.
Bedford
Muscatatuck
Madison
Vincennes
Washington
East Fork White
White
NATIONAL
Blue
Patoka
Jasper
Ohio
Jeffersonville
Patoka Lake
New Albany
Huntingburg
FOREST
KENTUCKY
Wabash
Mount Vernon
Evansville
Ohio

ILLINOIS

OHIO

THE MIDWEST

Iowa

Land & Water
Hawkeye Point and the Missouri and Mississippi Rivers are important land and water features of Iowa.

Statehood
Iowa became the 29th state in 1846.

People & Places
Iowa's population is 3,002,555. Des Moines is the state capital and the largest city.

Fun Fact
Iowa's nickname, the Hawkeye State, comes from chief Black Hawk, a Sauk Indian chief who started the Black Hawk War in 1832.

▲ Hogs outnumber people five to one in **Iowa**, which produces 25 percent of all hogs raised in the U.S.

Iowa State Flag

Wild Rose State Flower

American Goldfinch State Bird

SOUTH DAKOTA

Hawkeye Point +
1,670 ft
509 m
Highest point in Iowa

Big Sioux

• Sheldon

• Orange City

Le Mars • Cherokee •

Floyd

• Sioux City

Missouri

Little Sioux

• Onawa   Denison •

NEBRASKA

Boyer

Harlan •

DE SOTO N.W.R.

• Council Bluffs

• Glenwood

Missouri

Shenandoah •

Map Key
★ State capital
••• City or town
...... Boundary
National Wildlife Refuge

◀ A young boy dressed in a colorful traditional outfit prepares to participate in the Annual Meskwaki Indian Powwow near **Tama**, Iowa.

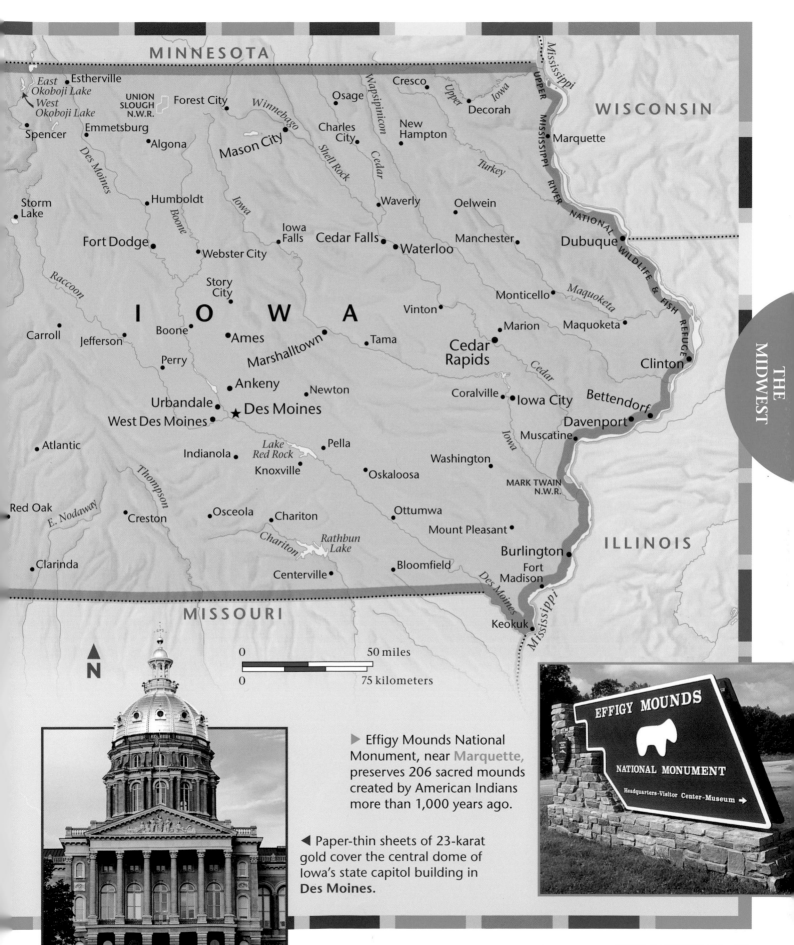

MINNESOTA

WISCONSIN

East Okoboji Lake
West Okoboji Lake

• Estherville
• Spencer
• Emmetsburg
• Algona
UNION SLOUGH N.W.R.
• Forest City

Winnebago
Mason City
• Cresco
• Osage
Charles City
• New Hampton
• Decorah
Upper Iowa
Marquette

Des Moines
Shell Rock
Cedar
Turkey

• Storm Lake
• Humboldt
• Fort Dodge
Boone
• Webster City
• Iowa Falls
• Waverly
Cedar Falls
• Oelwein
• Manchester
• Dubuque

MISSISSIPPI RIVER NATIONAL WILDLIFE & FISH REFUGE

Raccoon
Story City

I O W A

• Carroll
• Jefferson
• Boone
• Ames
• Tama
• Marion
Cedar Rapids
• Monticello
Maquoketa
• Maquoketa

Iowa
• Vinton

• Perry
Marshalltown
• Ankeny
• Newton
• Clinton

Cedar
• Coralville
• Iowa City
• Bettendorf

Urbandale
★ Des Moines
West Des Moines

• Atlantic
• Indianola
Lake Red Rock
• Pella
• Washington
• Davenport
• Muscatine

Thompson
Knoxville
• Oskaloosa

MARK TWAIN N.W.R.

• Red Oak
E. Nodaway
• Creston
• Osceola
• Chariton
• Ottumwa
• Mount Pleasant

• Clarinda
Chariton
Rathbun Lake
• Bloomfield
Burlington
Fort Madison

ILLINOIS

• Centerville

Des Moines

MISSOURI

Keokuk
Mississippi

N

0 ——— 50 miles
0 ——— 75 kilometers

▶ Effigy Mounds National Monument, near Marquette, preserves 206 sacred mounds created by American Indians more than 1,000 years ago.

◀ Paper-thin sheets of 23-karat gold cover the central dome of Iowa's state capitol building in Des Moines.

EFFIGY MOUNDS
NATIONAL MONUMENT
Headquarters-Visitor Center-Museum →

The Midwest

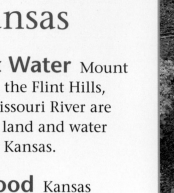

Kansas

Land & Water Mount Sunflower, the Flint Hills, and the Missouri River are important land and water features of Kansas.

Statehood Kansas became the 34th state in 1861.

People & Places The population of Kansas is 2,802,134. Topeka is the state capital. The largest city is Wichita.

Fun Fact Pizza Hut, the world's largest pizza chain, opened its first restaurant in Wichita in 1958. Today the company has branches in more than 100 countries.

▲ A statue of the Tin Man, a character from the popular 1939 fantasy movie *The Wizard of Oz*, which was set in Kansas, sits in a garden.

South Fork Republican
Beaver Creek
Sappa Creek
Goodland
Colby
Highest point in Kansas
COLORADO
+ Mt. Sunflower 4,039 ft 1,231 m
Oakley
Ladder Creek
White Woman Creek
Scott City
Arkansas
Lakin
Garden City
Bear Creek
Ulysses
North Fork
Cimarron
CIMARRON NAT. GRASSLAND
Liberal
HIGH PLAINS

Map Key

★ State capital
••• City or town
•••••• Boundary
Indian Reservation
National Preserve
National Grassland
National Wildlife Refuge

▼ The Chalk Pyramids are located in Gove County south of **Oakley**. These limestone formations were carved by erosion from the floor of an ancient inland sea.

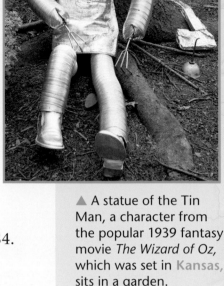

KANSAS

Kansas State Flag

Sunflower State Flower

Western Meadowlark State Bird

NEBRASKA

Norton
Phillipsburg
Prairie Dog Creek
Kirwin Reservoir
Lebanon
Belleville
Washington
Seneca
Little Blue
Big Blue
Marysville
SAC AND FOX I.R.
IOWA I.R.
Hiawatha

North Fork Solomon
KIRWIN N.W.R.
Waconda Lake
Concordia
Republican
Clay Center
Tuttle Creek Lake
KICKAPOO INDIAN RESERVATION
Holton
POTAWATOMI INDIAN RESERVATION
Atchison
Leavenworth

South Fork Solomon
Beloit
Solomon
Plainville
Manhattan
Wamego
Perry Lake
Kansas City
Overland Park

Smoky Hills
Minneapolis
Saline
Abilene
Milford Lake
Junction City
Kansas
Topeka ★

WaKeeney
Wilson Lake
Russell
Lawrence
Olathe

Cedar Bluff Reservoir
Hays
Salina
Smoky Hill
Hillsdale Lake

Smoky Hill
Ellsworth
Kanopolis Lake
Council Grove
Osage City
Ottawa

K A N S A S
Cheyenne Bottoms
McPherson
Neosho
Osawatomie

Ness City
Walnut Creek
Great Bend
Lyons
TALLGRASS PRAIRIE NATIONAL PRESERVE
Emporia
John Redmond Reservoir
Garnett
Marais des Cygnes

Pawnee
Larned
Arkansas
Marion Lake
FLINT HILLS N.W.R.
Burlington

QUIVIRA N.W.R.
Hesston
Newton
Verdigris
Iola

Buckner Creek
Kinsley
Hutchinson
El Dorado Lake
Eureka
Chanute
Fort Scott

Dodge City
Cheney Reservoir
Pratt
Wichita
El Dorado
Fall
Fredonia
Neosho
Pittsburg

Greensburg
Kingman
Derby
Flint Hills
Parsons

Crooked Creek
Red Hills
Medicine Lodge
Medicine Lodge
Wellington
Walnut
Winfield
Elk
Elk City Lake

Meade
Cimarron
Anthony
Arkansas City
Caney
Independence
Coffeyville
Baxter Springs

Missouri
MISSOURI

OKLAHOMA

THE MIDWEST

N

0 — 50 miles
0 — 75 kilometers

◀ People in carts and covered wagons reenact the westward movement through Kansas of traders and early settlers along the Santa Fe Trail following the **Missouri** and upper **Arkansas Rivers** towards Colorado and New Mexico.

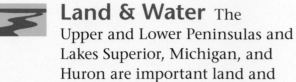

Michigan

Land & Water The Upper and Lower Peninsulas and Lakes Superior, Michigan, and Huron are important land and water features of Michigan.

Statehood Michigan became the 26th state in 1837.

People & Places Michigan's population is 10,003,422. Lansing is the state capital. The largest city is Detroit.

Fun Fact The record company Motown, named for Detroit's nickname "Motor City USA," grew from a small startup business in 1959 to one of the largest independent record companies in the world.

◀ A statue of Austin Blair, governor of Michigan during the Civil War, stands in front of the state capitol in **Lansing.**

◀ Boys explore nature's wonders on the bank of a river near **Niles.** The town sits on the site of Fort St. Joseph, built by the French in 1691.

▼ Snowmobiling is a popular winter sport on the **Upper Peninsula.** Michigan leads the U.S. in the number of registered snowmobiles. Many people also enjoy skiing and dog sledding.

Michigan State Flag

Apple Blossom State Flower

Robin State Bird

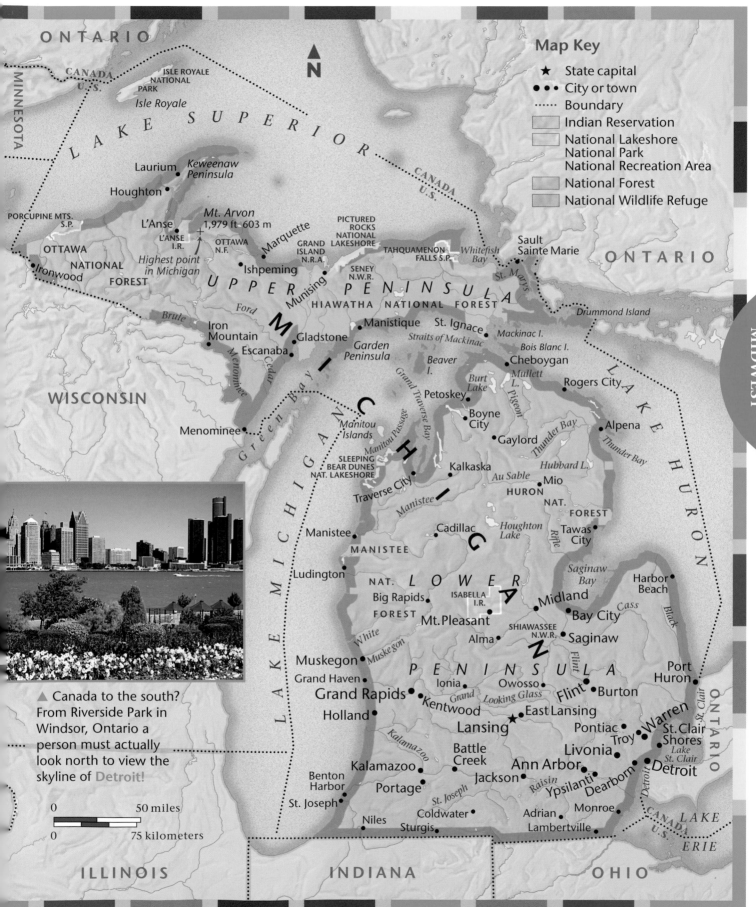

ONTARIO

MINNESOTA

CANADA
U.S.

ISLE ROYALE
NATIONAL
PARK

Isle Royale

N

Map Key

★ State capital
●●● City or town
···· Boundary
Indian Reservation
National Lakeshore
National Park
National Recreation Area
National Forest
National Wildlife Refuge

L A K E   S U P E R I O R

CANADA
U.S.

PORCUPINE MTS.
S.P.

Laurium
Keweenaw Peninsula

Houghton

L'Anse
L'ANSE
I.R.

Mt. Arvon
1,979 ft 603 m

OTTAWA
N.F.

Marquette

PICTURED
ROCKS
NATIONAL
LAKESHORE

GRAND
ISLAND
N.R.A.

TAHQUAMENON
FALLS S.P.

*Whitefish
Bay*

Sault
Sainte Marie

O N T A R I O

OTTAWA
NATIONAL
FOREST

Ironwood

*Highest point
in Michigan*

Ishpeming

Munising

SENEY
N.W.R.

St. Marys

U P P E R   P E N I N S U L A

H I A W A T H A   N A T I O N A L   F O R E S T

Drummond Island

WISCONSIN

Brule

Ford

Iron
Mountain

Gladstone

Manistique

St. Ignace

Mackinac I.

Straits of Mackinac

Bois Blanc I.

L
A
K
E

H
U
R
O
N

Escanaba

*Garden
Peninsula*

*Beaver
I.*

Cheboygan

Rogers City

Menominee

Cedar

Green Bay

Petoskey

*Burt
Lake*

*Mullett
L.*

Pigeon

Alpena

Menominee

M
I
C
H
I
G
A
N

*Manitou
Islands*

Grand Traverse Bay

Boyne
City

Gaylord

Thunder Bay

Thunder Bay

Manitou Passage

SLEEPING
BEAR DUNES
NAT. LAKESHORE

Kalkaska

Au Sable

Hubbard L.

Mio

Traverse City

Manistee

HURON

NAT.

*Houghton
Lake*

FOREST

Cadillac

Rifle

Tawas
City

Manistee

MANISTEE

*Saginaw
Bay*

Harbor
Beach

Ludington

NAT.

LOWER

ISABELLA
I.R.

Midland

Cass

FOREST

Big Rapids

Bay City

Black

Mt. Pleasant

SHIAWASSEE
N.W.R.

Saginaw

White

Alma

Muskegon

Muskegon

PENINSULA

Flint

Port
Huron

Grand Haven

Ionia

Owosso

Flint

Burton

O N T A R I O

Grand Rapids

Kentwood

Grand

Looking Glass

East Lansing

Holland

Lansing ★

Pontiac

St. Clair
Shores

Warren

Kalamazoo

Battle
Creek

Livonia

Troy

St. Clair

Benton
Harbor

Kalamazoo

Ann Arbor

Dearborn

Detroit

*Lake
St. Clair*

Portage

Jackson

Raisin

Ypsilanti

Detroit

St. Joseph

St. Joseph

Coldwater

Adrian

Monroe

CANADA
U.S.

LAKE

Niles

Sturgis

Lambertville

ERIE

ILLINOIS

INDIANA

OHIO

▲ Canada to the south?
From Riverside Park in
Windsor, Ontario a
person must actually
look north to view the
skyline of **Detroit!**

0   50 miles
0   75 kilometers

The Midwest

Minnesota

Land & Water Chippewa National Forest, Lake Superior, and the Mississippi River are important land and water features of Minnesota.

Statehood Minnesota became the 32nd state in 1858.

People & Places Minnesota's population is 5,220,393. St. Paul is the state capital. The largest city is Minneapolis.

Fun Fact Modern in-line skates were invented by two Minnesota students. Looking for a way to practice hockey in the summer, they replaced their skate blades with wheels.

◀ Minnesota's gray wolf population is growing and no longer endangered thanks to the work of the International Wolf Center in **Ely**.

▼ Some people in **Minnesota** sit for hours in "ice shacks" and fish through holes cut in the ice of frozen lakes.

Minnesota State Flag

Showy Lady's Slipper
State Flower

Common Loon
State Bird

The "Northwest Angle" is the northernmost point in the 48 contiguous states

RED LAKE INDIAN RES.

MANITOBA

CANADA
U.S.

Roseau

Hallock

Lake of the Woods

Baudette

Rainy Lake

Map Key

★ State capital
●●● City or town
····· Boundary

Indian Reservation
National Park
National Riverway
National Forest
National Wildlife Refuge

International Falls

Rainy

VOYAGEURS NATIONAL PARK

Namakan Lake

ONTARIO

Highest point in Minnesota

CANADA

Pigeon

U.S.

AGASSIZ N.W.R.

Mud Lake

Roseau

RED LAKE INDIAN RES.

Big Fork

BOIS FORTE I.R.

BOUNDARY WATERS CANOE AREA WILDERNESS

Eagle Mt. 2,301 ft 701 m

GRAND PORTAGE I.R.

Thief River Falls

Red Lake

RED LAKE INDIAN RESERVATION

Upper Red Lake

Vermilion Lake

BOIS FORTE (DEER CREEK) I.R.

Ely SUPERIOR

Grand Marais

Crookston

Lower Red Lake

Mesabi Range

Virginia

NATIONAL

LAKE SUPERIOR

MICHIGAN

Red Lake

Source of the Mississippi River

Red Lake

Winnibigoshish Lake

CHIPPEWA

NATIONAL

LEECH LAKE INDIAN RES.

FOREST

Hibbing

Grand Rapids

Two Harbors

Bemidji

Mississippi

WHITE EARTH INDIAN RESERVATION

Lake Itasca

Leech Lake

FOREST

Duluth

St. Louis

FOND DU LAC I.R.

Proctor

NORTH DAKOTA

Red River of the North

Wild Rice

HAMDEN SLOUGH N.W.R.

TAMARAC N.W.R.

Park Rapids

Cloquet

Mississippi

RICE LAKE N.W.R.

Moorhead

Detroit Lakes

Crow Wing

Pelican Rapids

Wadena

Otter Tail Lake

Brainerd

Mille Lacs Lake

Fergus Falls

Otter Tail

MINNESOTA

Sandstone

St. Croix

ST. CROIX NATIONAL SCENIC RIVERWAY

Bois de Sioux

Little Falls

MILLE LACS I.R.

Mora

Lake Traverse

Alexandria

Milaca

Morris

Chippewa

Rum

WISCONSIN

Big Stone Lake

St. Cloud

N. Fork

Mississippi

SHERBURNE N.W.R.

N

Ortonville

Benson

Crow

Brooklyn Park

Coon Rapids

Willmar

Litchfield

Stillwater

Montevideo

S. Fork

Minneapolis

★ St. Paul

Hutchinson

Crow

Bloomington

Eagan

SOUTH DAKOTA

Minnesota

LOWER SIOUX I.R.

Lakeville

Lake Pepin

Redwood Falls

Red Wing

Marshall

Northfield

UPPER MISSISSIPPI RIVER

New Ulm

Faribault

Mankato

Owatonna

Winona

NATIONAL

Pipestone

St. James

Waseca

Rochester

WILDLIFE

Slayton

Preston

AND

Luverne

Worthington

Blue Earth

Albert Lea

Austin

Root

Mississippi

FISH

Des Moines

Fairmont

REFUGE

IOWA

◄ The skyline of Minneapolis rises above Lake Harriet, part of the Chain of Lakes and a popular recreation area.

0 ——— 50 miles
0 ——— 150 kilometers

▲ A young woman, dressed in the traditional costume of an Indian princess, prepares to join the dancing at the **Minneapolis** Powwow.

THE MIDWEST

Missouri

Land & Water

Mark Twain National Forest and the Missouri and Mississippi Rivers are important land and water features of Missouri.

Statehood
Missouri became the 24th state in 1821.

People & Places

Missouri's population is 5,911,605. Jefferson City is the state capital. The largest city is Kansas City.

Fun Fact
Mark Twain's childhood in Hannibal, a town on the Mississippi River, inspired many of his books, including *The Adventures of Tom Sawyer* and *The Adventures of Huckleberry Finn*.

Missouri State Flag

Eastern Bluebird
State Bird

Hawthorn
State Flower

▲ In 1804, the Lewis and Clark Expedition set off from St. Charles, Missouri, to explore the Northwest Territories. In 2004 the bicentennial of this important event was celebrated.

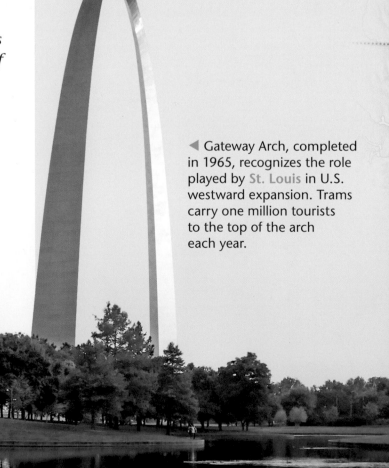

◀ Gateway Arch, completed in 1965, recognizes the role played by St. Louis in U.S. westward expansion. Trams carry one million tourists to the top of the arch each year.

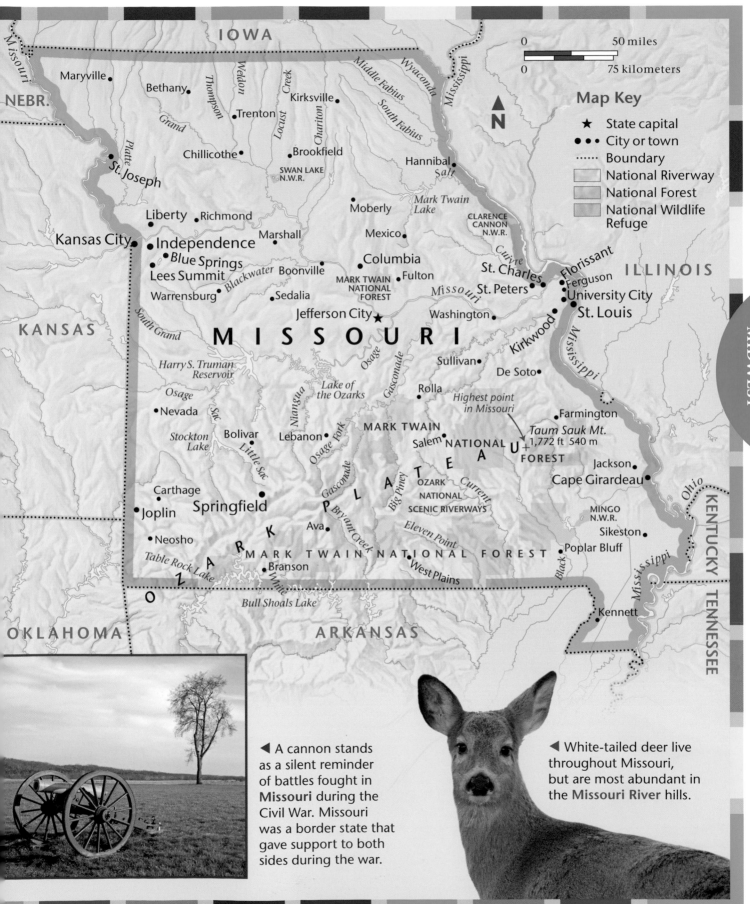

IOWA

NEBR.

Missouri

Maryville

Bethany

Thompson

Weldon

Grand

Kirksville

Trenton

Locust Creek

Chariton

Middle Fabius

Wyaconda

Mississippi

Chillicothe

Brookfield

South Fabius

Hannibal

Salt

SWAN LAKE N.W.R.

Mark Twain Lake

CLARENCE CANNON N.W.R.

Moberly

St. Joseph

Platte

Liberty

Richmond

Mexico

Kansas City

Independence

Marshall

Columbia

Cuivre

St. Charles

Florissant

ILLINOIS

Blue Springs

Boonville

Fulton

St. Peters

Ferguson

Lees Summit

Blackwater

MARK TWAIN NATIONAL FOREST

Missouri

St. Louis

University City

Warrensburg

Sedalia

Washington

Kirkwood

Jefferson City ★

M I S S O U R I

South Grand

Osage

Sullivan

De Soto

Mississippi

Harry S. Truman Reservoir

Lake of the Ozarks

Gasconade

Rolla

Highest point in Missouri

Farmington

Osage

Nevada

Sac

Niangua

MARK TWAIN

Taum Sauk Mt. 1,772 ft 540 m

Stockton Lake

Bolivar

Little Sac

Lebanon

Osage Fork

Salem

NATIONAL

FOREST

Jackson

Carthage

Gasconade

Big Piney

OZARK NATIONAL SCENIC RIVERWAYS

Current

Cape Girardeau

Joplin

Springfield

Ava

Bryant Creek

Eleven Point

MINGO N.W.R.

Sikeston

Neosho

Table Rock Lake

M A R K   T W A I N   N A T I O N A L   F O R E S T

West Plains

Poplar Bluff

Branson

White

Black

Mississippi

KANSAS

O   Z   A   R   K   P   L   A   T   E   A   U

Bull Shoals Lake

Kennett

OKLAHOMA

ARKANSAS

Ohio

KENTUCKY

TENNESSEE

0   50 miles

0   75 kilometers

Map Key

★ State capital

●●● City or town

⋯⋯ Boundary

National Riverway

National Forest

National Wildlife Refuge

◄ A cannon stands as a silent reminder of battles fought in **Missouri** during the Civil War. Missouri was a border state that gave support to both sides during the war.

◄ White-tailed deer live throughout Missouri, but are most abundant in the **Missouri River** hills.

Nebraska

Land & Water
Panorama Point and the Platte and Missouri Rivers are important land and water features of Nebraska.

Statehood
Nebraska became the 37th state in 1867.

People & Places
Nebraska's population is 1,783,432. Lincoln is the state capital. The largest city is Omaha.

Fun Fact
The largest remaining area of original native prairie in the United States is in the Sand Hills region. It is an important stopover for migrating sandhill cranes.

Nebraska State Flag

Goldenrod State Flower

Western Meadowlark State Bird

▶ Two black-tailed prairie dogs watch for signs of danger at the entrance to their burrow in the **Fort Niobrara National Wildlife Refuge.**

OGLALA NATIONAL GRASSLAND

Chadron

Crawford

White Pine Ridge

Gordon

NEBRASKA • Rushville

NATIONAL FOREST

WYOMING

Alliance

Sand

Scottsbluff

Gering

Bayard

CRESCENT LAKE N.W.R.

Bridgeport

Pumpkin Creek

North Platte

Highest point in Nebraska

Lake C.W. McConaughy

Kimball

Lodgepole Cr. • Sidney

▼ Panorama Point
+ 5,423 ft, 1,653 m

South Platte • Ogallala

COLORADO

• Grant

• Imperia

Frenchman C

▼ Tourists dressed like Indians and pioneers participate in a reenactment of a 19th-century wagon train under attack by Indians while traveling along the Oregon Trail through Nebraska near **Bayard.**

Map Key

★ State capital
●●● City or town
····· Boundary

	Indian Reservation
	National Forest
	National Grassland
	National Wildlife Refuge

SOUTH DAKOTA

▲ In recent years, annual snowfall in **Lincoln** has averaged more than 30 inches (76 cm), creating work for adults but fun for kids.

Valentine
Niobrara
FORT NIOBRARA N.W.R.
SAMUEL R. McKELVIE NATIONAL FOREST
Gordon Cr.
VALENTINE N.W.R.
Keya Paha
Niobrara
Ainsworth
Atkinson
O'Neill
Holt Creek
Lewis and Clark Lake
SANTEE INDIAN RES.
Hartington
South Sioux City
WINNEBAGO I.R.
OMAHA I.R.
IOWA

H i l l s
Mullen
NEBRASKA NAT. FOREST
Dismal
North Loup
Calamus
Middle Loup
Calamus Reservoir
Burwell
Elkhorn
Neligh
Norfolk
Madison
Verdigre Cr.
Logan Creek
Tekamah
Blair

N E B R A S K A
South Loup
Broken Bow
Cedar
Shell Cr.
Columbus
Fremont
Omaha
Wahoo
Papillion
Bellevue
Platte
Plattsmouth

North Platte
Platte
Gothenburg
Lexington
Kearney
Ravenna
St. Paul
Grand Island
Central City
Aurora
Fullerton
Loup
Big Blue
York
Seward
Waverly
★Lincoln
Nebraska City
Crete

Red Willow Creek
Hugh Butler Lake
Cambridge
Republican
Holdrege
Minden
Hastings
Geneva
Little Blue
Big Nemaha
Auburn
Missouri
Beatrice
Fairbury
Falls City

Swanson Res.
McCook
Alma
Harlan County Lake
Red Cloud
Superior

MISSOURI

SAC AND FOX I.R. IOWA I.R.

KANSAS

N

0   50 miles
0   75 kilometers

▶ Old cars balanced on top of concrete pillars form a creative replica of the famous Stonehenge site in Great Britain. This unusual monument, called Carhenge, is located near **Alliance**.

North Dakota

Land & Water The Great Plains, the Badlands, and the Missouri River are important land and water features of North Dakota.

Statehood North Dakota became the 39th state in 1889.

People & Places North Dakota's population is 641,481. Bismarck is the state capital. The largest city is Fargo.

Fun Fact North Dakota leads the country in production of sunflower seeds—more than a billion pounds each year. Sunflowers grow as tall as 13 feet (4 m).

▲ North Dakota's sedimentary rocks offered ideal conditions for formation of fossils such as this leaf.

▲ Cowboys on the fence watch the excitement of the rodeo during the Slope County Fair in Amidon.

North Dakota State Flag

Wild Prairie Rose State Flower

Western Meadowlark State Bird

◄ American bison are native to the Great Plains, but now are found mainly in parks such as Sullys Hill National Game Preserve in North Dakota.

CANADA
U.S.
SASKATCHE
Crosby

MONTANA

Little Muddy
Tioga
White Earth
Williston
Missouri

LITTLE
Watford City
THEODORE ROOSEVELT N.P. (NORTH UNIT)
Little Missouri

MISSOURI
THEODORE ROOSEVELT N.P. (ELKHORN RANCH SITE)

Yellowstone

Badlands

NATIONAL
THEODORE ROOSEVELT N.P. (SOUTH UNIT)
Medora
Dickinson

GRASSLAND
Amidon
+ White Butte
3,506 ft
1,069 m

Little Missouri
Bowman
Cedar
Hettinger

0 ——— 100 miles
0 ——— 150 kilometers

N

MANITOBA

CANADA
U.S.

Portal

SWAN

DES LACS
N.W.R.

Kenmare

UPPER
SOURIS
N.W.R.

LOSTWOOD
N.W.R.

Lake Darling

Stanley

Minot

New
Town

FORT BERTHOLD

Lake Sakakawea

INDIAN

RESERVATION

Garrison

Beulah

Knife

Center

Glen Ullin

Mandan

★ Bismarck

*Lake
Tschida*

Heart

*Lake
Oahe*

Mott

*Highest point
in North Dakota*

STANDING

CEDAR RIVER
NATIONAL GRASSLAND

ROCK

Fort Yates

INDIAN

RESERVATION

SOUTH DAKOTA

J. CLARK
SALYER
N.W.R.

Turtle Mts.

TURTLE
MT. I.R.

Rolla

Langdon

D r i f t   P r a i r i e

Cando

Rugby

Towner

*Souris
(Mouse)*

LAKE ALICE
N.W.R.

Dry Lake

Sweetwater Lake

Devils Lake

SULLYS HILL
NATIONAL GAME PRESERVE

*Stump
Lake*

SPIRIT LAKE
DAKOTAH
NATION

Harvey

Sheyenne

James

New
Rockford

AUDUBON N.W.R.

*Audubon
Lake*

Washburn

Missouri

GREAT

Cooperstown

Northwood

ARROWWOOD
N.W.R.

*Horsehead
Lake*

Pipestem Creek

CHASE LAKE
N.W.R.

*Jamestown
Reservoir*

Jamestown

Steele

Long Lake

LONG LAKE
N.W.R.

Napoleon

Beaver Creek

Linton

Wishek

Ashley

Ellendale

James

Maple

LaMoure

Oakes

Pembina

Pembina

Drayton

Grafton

Park River

Park

Grand Forks

Mayville

Hillsboro

*Lake
Ashtabula*

Valley
City

Casselton

West Fargo

Maple

Fargo

Red River of the North

MINNESOTA

Sheyenne

SHEYENNE
NATIONAL
GRASSLAND

Wild Rice

Wahpeton

TEWAUKON
N.W.R.

LAKE
TRAVERSE
(SISSETON)
INDIAN
RESERVATION

N O R T H   D A K O T A

GREAT   PLAINS

Cannonball

Creek

Map Key

★ State capital
••• City or town
······ Boundary
Indian Reservation
National Park
National Grassland
National Wildlife Refuge

◀ Painted Canyon stretches as far as
the eye can see at **Theodore Roosevelt
National Park.** The park is a living
memorial to the 26th President and
home to many animal species from wild
horses to snapping turtles.

The Midwest

Ohio

Land & Water Wayne National Forest, Lake Erie, and the Ohio River are important land and water features of Ohio.

Statehood Ohio became the 17th state in 1803.

People & Places Ohio's population is 11,485,910. Columbus is the state capital and the largest city.

? **Fun Fact** Ohio's nick-name, the Buckeye State, comes from a local tree. The tree's common name was derived from the Native Americans, who thought its seeds looked like the eye of a male deer, or buck.

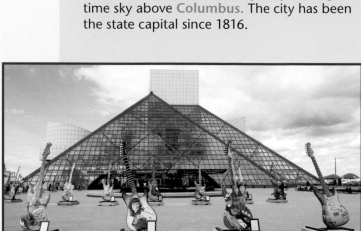
▲ Fourth of July fireworks light up the night-time sky above **Columbus**. The city has been the state capital since 1816.

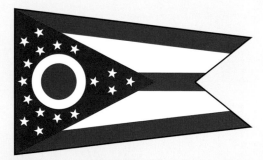
▲ Colorful guitars mark the entrance to the Rock and Roll Hall of Fame, established in downtown **Cleveland** in 1995.

▼ The Blue Streak is the oldest operating roller coaster at Cedar Point Amusement Park in **Sandusky**. This popular ride is named after a local high school sports team.

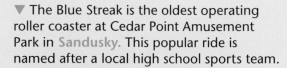

Ohio State Flag

Scarlet Carnation State Flower

Cardinal State Bird

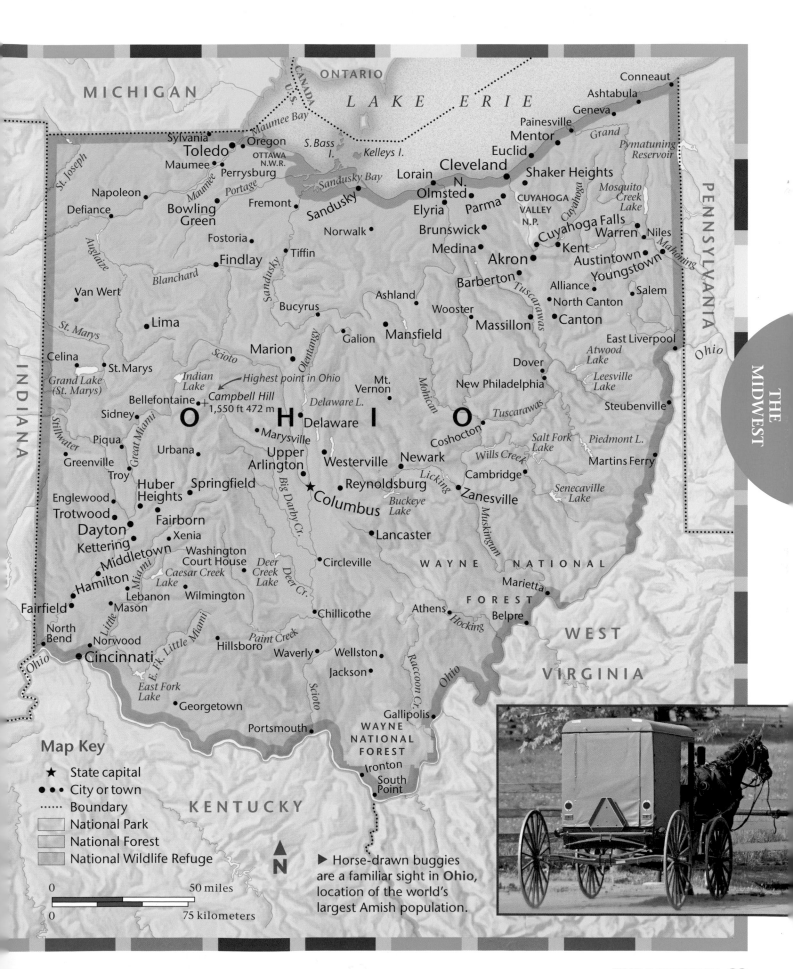

MICHIGAN

ONTARIO

CANADA
U.S.

LAKE ERIE

Conneaut
Ashtabula
Geneva

Maumee Bay
Sylvania
Oregon
Toledo
Maumee
Perrysburg
Napoleon
Defiance
Bowling
Green
Fremont
Portage
S. Bass
I.
Kelleys I.

OTTAWA
N.W.R.

Sandusky Bay

Lorain
N.
Olmsted
Elyria

Cleveland
Painesville
Mentor
Euclid
Shaker Heights

Grand
Pymatuning
Reservoir

Mosquito
Creek
Lake

Parma
Cuyahoga
Brunswick
Medina

CUYAHOGA
VALLEY
N.P.

Cuyahoga Falls
Warren
Niles
Kent

Mahoning

St. Joseph

Van Wert

Napoleon
Defiance

Auglaize

Blanchard

Fostoria
Findlay
Tiffin

Sandusky

Norwalk

Bucyrus

Ashland
Wooster

Akron
Barberton
Massillon

Austintown
Youngstown
Alliance
North Canton
Canton

Salem

Tuscarawas

East Liverpool

Lima
St. Marys

St. Marys

Celina
Grand Lake
(St. Marys)
St. Marys

Indian
Lake

Bellefontaine

Sidney

Piqua
Greenville
Troy

Englewood
Trotwood
Dayton
Kettering
Huber
Heights
Fairborn
Middletown
Hamilton
Xenia
Springfield

Washington
Court House

Lebanon
Mason
Wilmington

Fairfield

North
Bend
Norwood
Cincinnati

Ohio

Georgetown

East Fork
Lake

E. Fk. Little Miami

Hillsboro

Portsmouth

KENTUCKY

Marion

Galion

Scioto

Olentangy

Mansfield

Mt.
Vernon

Delaware L.

Mohican

OHIO

Delaware
Marysville
Upper
Arlington
Westerville
Reynoldsburg

Columbus

Big Darby Cr.

Deer Cr.

Deer
Creek
Lake

Caesar Creek
Lake

Circleville

Chillicothe

Paint Creek

Waverly

Wellston

Jackson

Scioto

Buckeye
Lake

Newark

Coshocton

Licking

Cambridge

Zanesville

Wills Creek

Senecaville
Lake

Muskingum

Lancaster

WAYNE

FOREST

Athens

Hocking

Raccoon Cr.

Gallipolis

WAYNE
NATIONAL
FOREST

Ironton
South
Point

Highest point in Ohio
Campbell Hill
1,550 ft 472 m

O

O

Dover

New Philadelphia

Tuscarawas

Atwood
Lake

Leesville
Lake

Salt Fork
Lake

Piedmont L.

Steubenville

Martins Ferry

NATIONAL

Marietta

Belpre

WEST

VIRGINIA

Ohio

PENNSYLVANIA

OHIO

THE
MIDWEST

INDIANA

Map Key

★ State capital
••• City or town
⋯⋯ Boundary
National Park
National Forest
National Wildlife Refuge

0   50 miles

0   75 kilometers

N

▶ Horse-drawn buggies
are a familiar sight in **Ohio**,
location of the world's
largest Amish population.

South Dakota

Land & Water The Black Hills, National Grasslands, and the Missouri River are important land and water features of South Dakota.

Statehood South Dakota became the 40th state in 1889.

People & Places South Dakota's population is 804,194. Pierre is the state capital. The largest city is Sioux Falls.

Fun Fact The world's largest, most complete, and best preserved specimen of *Tyrannosaurus rex,* nicknamed Sue, was unearthed on the Cheyenne River Sioux Indian Reservation in 1990.

▲ A mountain cotton-tail nibbles on some grass in **Wind Cave National Park.**

◀ A funny sign warns South Dakota motorists of a dinosaur crossing.

South Dakota State Flag

Pasqueflower State Flower

Ring-Necked Pheasant State Bird

▼ Carvings on **Mount Rushmore** in the Black Hills honor four past presidents (from left to right): George Washington, Thomas Jefferson, Theodore Roosevelt, and Abraham Lincoln.

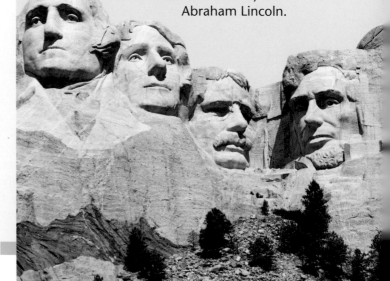

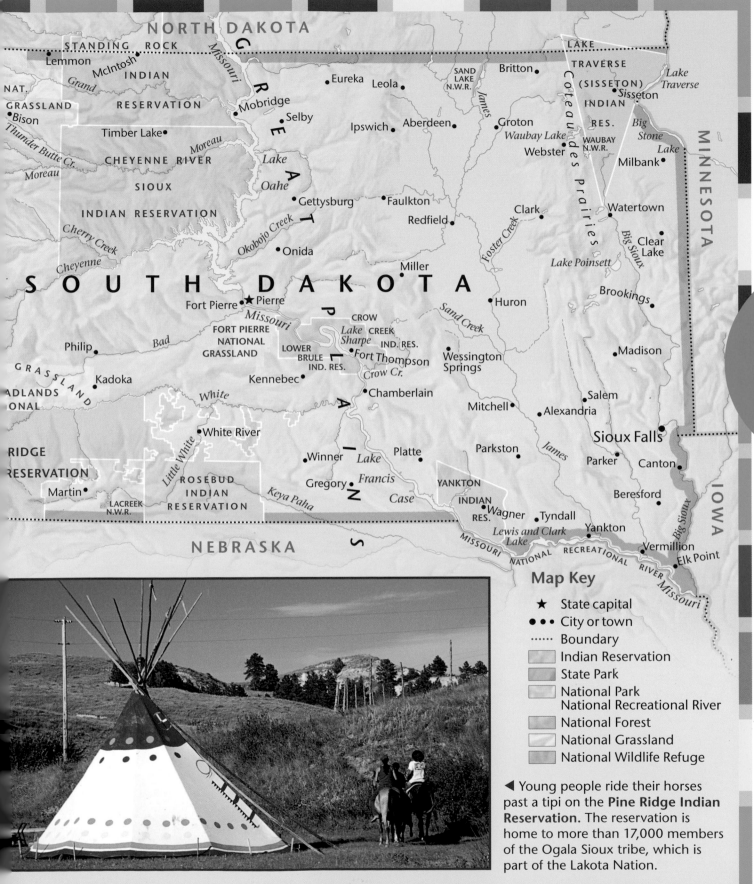

NORTH DAKOTA

STANDING ROCK INDIAN RESERVATION

Lemmon
McIntosh
NAT. GRASSLAND
Bison
Thunder Butte Cr.
Grand
Timber Lake
Moreau
CHEYENNE RIVER
Moreau
SIOUX
INDIAN RESERVATION
Cherry Creek
Cheyenne
Eureka
Leola
Mobridge
Selby
Ipswich
Aberdeen
Lake Oahe
Gettysburg
Faulkton
Redfield
Okobojo Creek
Onida
Miller

SAND LAKE N.W.R.
Britton
James
Groton
Waubay Lake
Webster
WAUBAY N.W.R.

LAKE TRAVERSE (SISSETON) INDIAN RES.
Lake Traverse
Sisseton
Big Stone Lake
Milbank

MINNESOTA

Clark
Coteau des prairies
Watertown
Foster Creek
Lake Poinsett
Big Sioux
Clear Lake

S O U T H   D A K O T A

Fort Pierre ★ Pierre
Missouri
Bad
FORT PIERRE NATIONAL GRASSLAND
CROW CREEK IND. RES.
Lake Sharpe
LOWER BRULE IND. RES.
Fort Thompson
Crow Cr.
Sand Creek
Wessington Springs
Huron
Brookings
Madison

GRASSLAND
Philip
Kadoka
BADLANDS ONAL
Kennebec
White
White River
Chamberlain
Mitchell
Alexandria
Salem
Parker
Canton

RIDGE RESERVATION
Martin
LACREEK N.W.R.
Little White
ROSEBUD INDIAN RESERVATION
Keya Paha
Winner
Gregory
Lake Francis
Platte
Case
Parkston
James
Beresford
Big Sioux

YANKTON INDIAN RES.
Wagner
Tyndall
Yankton
Lewis and Clark Lake
Vermillion
Elk Point
MISSOURI NATIONAL RECREATIONAL RIVER
Missouri

Sioux Falls

IOWA

NEBRASKA

G R E A T   P L A I N S

Map Key

★ State capital
••• City or town
⋯⋯ Boundary
▢ Indian Reservation
▢ State Park
▢ National Park
National Recreational River
▢ National Forest
▢ National Grassland
▢ National Wildlife Refuge

◀ Young people ride their horses past a tipi on the **Pine Ridge Indian Reservation**. The reservation is home to more than 17,000 members of the Ogala Sioux tribe, which is part of the Lakota Nation.

The Midwest

Wisconsin

Land & Water Apostle Islands, Green Bay, and Lakes Superior and Michigan are important land and water features of Wisconsin.

Statehood Wisconsin became the 30th state in 1848.

People & Places Wisconsin's population is 5,627,967. Madison is the state capital. The largest city is Milwaukee.

Fun Fact Laura Ingalls Wilder was born in Pepin in 1867. Her famous "Little House" books are based on her childhood in the forests and prairies of the Midwest.

▲ In **Wisconsin** the bald eagle is found only in the northern regions.

◄ A young Native American man dressed in colorful traditional costume dances at a festival in Milwaukee.

▲ In a winter version of sailing, ice boats compete in a race on the frozen surface of Lake Winnebago near Oshkosh.

WISCONSIN
1848
Wisconsin State Flag

Robin
State Bird

Wood Violet
State Flower

LAKE SUPERIOR

APOSTLE ISLANDS NATIONAL LAKESHORE
Apostle Islands
RED CLIFF I.R.
Madeline Island

Superior

CHEQUAMEGON-
Ashland
BAD RIVER INDIAN RES.

Bois Brule

St. Croix

▶ Wisconsin produces more than 600 types of cheese. The town of **Monroe** celebrates "Cheese Days" each year.

NICOLET
Turtle-Flambeau Flowage
LAC DU FLAMBEAU INDIAN RES.

Wisconsin

Brule

CHEQUAMEGON-

MICHIGAN

Hayward
Lake Chippewa
Eagle River

NICOLET

Pine
Popple
Menominee

ST. CROIX
NATIONAL
Namekagon
LAC COURTE OREILLES I.R.
Park Falls
Chippewa
SCENIC
Spooner
NATIONAL
Rhinelander

NATIONAL

Peshtigo

Washington Island

RIVERWAY
Rice Lake
Ladysmith

Highest point in Wisconsin
Tomahawk

FOREST

Wolf

FOREST

Marinette

St. Croix
St. Croix Falls
Flambeau
Jump
Timms Hill
1,951ft
595 m
Merrill
Antigo

Oconto

Green Bay

Apple
Red Cedar
Yellow
Medford
Wausau
MENOMINEE INDIAN RES.

Oconto
Door Peninsula
Sturgeon Bay

Hudson
River Falls
Chippewa Falls
Lake Wissota
Big Eau Pleine Reservoir
STOCKBRIDGE I.R.
Shawano

Menomonie
Eau Claire
Marshfield
Lake Du Bay

WISCONSIN

ONEIDA INDIAN RES.
Green Bay
De Pere

Lake Pepin
Chippewa
Stevens Point
Wisconsin
Appleton
Kaukauna

Mississippi
Pepin
Black River Falls
Wisconsin Rapids
Wolf
Neenah
Two Rivers

Black
NECEDAH N.W.R.
Petenwell Lake
Lake Poygan
Oshkosh
Lake Winnebago
Manitowoc

Sparta
Castle Rock Lake

LAKE

Onalaska
Tomah
Fond du Lac
Sheboygan

La Crosse
Waupun
HORICON N.W.R.
MICHIGAN

Kickapoo
Baraboo
Portage
Beaver Dam
West Bend
Port Washington

Viroqua
Lake Wisconsin
Menomonee Falls
Wauwatosa

Wisconsin
Sun Prairie
Watertown
Brookfield
West Allis
Milwaukee

Prairie du Chien
Lake Mendota
Madison ★
Waukesha

Stoughton

Platteville
Pecatonica
Monroe
Sugar
Whitewater
Janesville
Racine

Rock
Beloit
Kenosha

Mississippi

MINNESOTA

IOWA

UPPER MISSISSIPPI RIVER NATIONAL WILDLIFE AND FISH REFUGE

ILLINOIS

Map Key

★ State capital
••• City or town
· · · · Boundary
  Indian Reservation
  National Lakeshore
  National Scenic Riverway
  National Forest
  National Wildlife Refuge

◀ Wisconsin has more dairy farms than any other state, earning it the nickname "America's Dairyland." The state dairy council is located in Brookfield.

0   50 miles
0   150 kilometers

THE MIDWEST

The Southwest

The Southwest region extends from the humid Gulf Coast in the east to the arid canyonlands in the west. The people of the region are just as varied as the natural landscape. Native Americans, descendants of early Spanish settlers, and recent immigrants from Mexico and Central America contribute to this region's special cultural landscape. Agriculture, cattle ranching, and the oil industry are traditional economic activities. The Southwest is a part of the Sunbelt where rapid population growth and sprawling cities are putting pressure on the region's limited water resources.

A rainbow frames Cerro Castellon in Big Bend National Park. This eroded mount of volcanic rock rises almost 3,300 feet (1,006 m) above the desert floor. Raising horses is a part of the cultural tradition in this region.

The Southwest

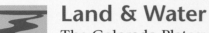

Arizona

Land & Water
The Colorado Plateau, the Grand Canyon, and the Colorado River are important land and water features of Arizona.

Statehood
Arizona became the 48th state in 1912.

People & Places
Arizona's population is 6,500,180. Phoenix is the state capital and the largest city.

Fun Fact
Of the 21 Indian reservations in Arizona, the largest belongs to the Navajo Nation. Native peoples and the federal government own 70 percent of the state.

▲ Daring boaters get soaked as they run the rapids on the fast flowing waters of the **Colorado River** in Grand Canyon National Park.

▶ Saguaro cacti, found in the Sonoran Desert, can grow to more than 30 feet (9 m).

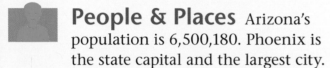
Arizona State Flag

Cactus Wren State Bird

Saguaro State Flower

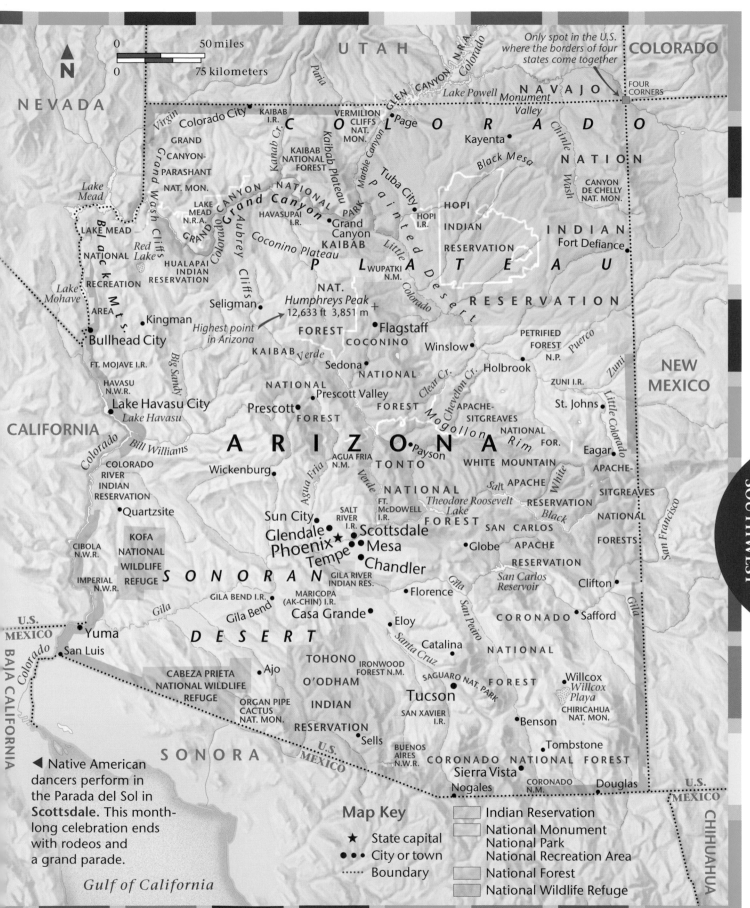

N

| 0 | 50 miles |
| 0 | 75 kilometers |

UTAH

COLORADO

NEVADA

Only spot in the U.S. where the borders of four states come together

FOUR CORNERS

N A V A J O

GLEN CANYON N.R.A.

Lake Powell

Colorado

Monument Valley

Virgin

Paria

Colorado City

KAIBAB I.R.

VERMILION CLIFFS NAT. MON.

Page

Kayenta

Chinle

N A T I O N

GRAND CANYON-PARASHANT NAT. MON.

Kanab Cr.

KAIBAB NATIONAL FOREST

Kaibab Plateau

Marble Canyon

Tuba City

Black Mesa

Wash

CANYON DE CHELLY NAT. MON.

I N D I A N

Lake Mead

LAKE MEAD N.R.A.

GRAND CANYON

Opatki

Colorado

HAVASUPAI I.R.

Grand Canyon

HOPI I.R.

HOPI INDIAN RESERVATION

Fort Defiance

LAKE MEAD NATIONAL RECREATION AREA

Black

Red Lake

HUALAPAI INDIAN RESERVATION

Aubrey

Coconino Plateau

KAIBAB

Little Colorado

WUPATKI N.M.

Colorado

R E S E R V A T I O N

Lake Mohave

Mts.

Seligman

NAT.

Humphreys Peak 12,633 ft 3,851 m +

FOREST

Painted Desert

P L A T E A U

Kingman

Highest point in Arizona

Flagstaff

COCONINO

Winslow

PETRIFIED FOREST N.P.

Puerco

NEW MEXICO

Bullhead City

FT. MOJAVE I.R.

HAVASU N.W.R.

Big Sandy

KAIBAB

Verde

Sedona

NATIONAL

Holbrook

Clear Cr.

Chevelon Cr.

ZUNI I.R.

Zuni

St. Johns

Little Colorado

Lake Havasu City

Lake Havasu

NATIONAL

Prescott Valley

FOREST

APACHE-SITGREAVES NATIONAL FOR.

Eagar

CALIFORNIA

Colorado

Bill Williams

Prescott

FOREST

Mogollon Rim

A R I Z O N A

Agua Fria

AGUA FRIA N.M.

Payson

TONTO

WHITE MOUNTAIN

Salt

APACHE

White

APACHE-SITGREAVES

COLORADO RIVER INDIAN RESERVATION

Wickenburg

Agua Fria

Verde

NATIONAL

FT. McDOWELL I.R.

Theodore Roosevelt Lake

RESERVATION

Black

NATIONAL FORESTS

San Francisco

Quartzsite

KOFA NATIONAL WILDLIFE REFUGE

Sun City

Glendale

SALT RIVER I.R.

Scottsdale

FOREST

SAN CARLOS

CIBOLA N.W.R.

Phoenix

Mesa

Globe

APACHE

Clifton

Tempe

Chandler

RESERVATION

IMPERIAL N.W.R.

S O N O R A N

GILA RIVER INDIAN RES.

Gila

San Carlos Reservoir

Safford

Gila

Florence

CORONADO

U.S. MEXICO

Colorado

Yuma

Gila

GILA BEND I.R.

MARICOPA (AK-CHIN) I.R.

Casa Grande

Eloy

San Pedro

NATIONAL

Gila

San Luis

Gila Bend

D E S E R T

Catalina

Santa Cruz

FOREST

BAJA CALIFORNIA

CABEZA PRIETA NATIONAL WILDLIFE REFUGE

Ajo

TOHONO

IRONWOOD FOREST N.M.

SAGUARO NAT PARK

Willcox

Willcox Playa

O'ODHAM

SAN XAVIER I.R.

Tucson

CHIRICAHUA NAT. MON.

ORGAN PIPE CACTUS NAT. MON.

INDIAN

Benson

RESERVATION

Sells

BUENOS AIRES N.W.R.

Tombstone

S O N O R A

U.S. MEXICO

CORONADO NATIONAL FOREST

Sierra Vista

Nogales

CORONADO N.M.

Douglas

U.S. MEXICO

CHIHUAHUA

◄ Native American dancers perform in the Parada del Sol in **Scottsdale**. This month-long celebration ends with rodeos and a grand parade.

Gulf of California

Map Key

★ State capital

••• City or town

•••• Boundary

☐ Indian Reservation

☐ National Monument
National Park
National Recreation Area

☐ National Forest

☐ National Wildlife Refuge

The Southwest

New Mexico

Land & Water The Sangre de Cristo Mountains, Carlsbad Caverns, and the Rio Grande are important land and water features of New Mexico.

Statehood New Mexico became the 47th state in 1912.

People & Places New Mexico's population is 1,984,356. Santa Fe is the state capital. The largest city is Albuquerque.

Fun Fact Roswell is a popular destination for people interested in UFOs. A local rancher discovered what he believed to be wreckage of a UFO in 1947.

▲ Brightly colored balloons rise into a blue sky in **Albuquerque** during the International Balloon Fiesta, the largest such event in the world.

◀ The caves of **Carlsbad Caverns** were created as natural sulfuric acid dissolved the limestone rocks.

▼ Chili peppers, seen here in a store in **Santa Fe**, give Southwestern food a distinctive taste. New Mexico is the leading U.S. producer of chilies.

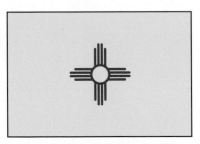

New Mexico State Flag

Yucca State Flower

Roadrunner State Bird

Only spot in the U.S. where the borders of four states come together

UT.

NAVAJO

NATION

INDIAN

RESERVATION

ARIZONA

APACHE-SITGREAVES

NATIONAL FOR.

COLORADO

FOUR CORNERS

UTE MOUNTAIN I.R.

San Juan

San Juan

Shiprock

Farmington

Aztec

Bloomfield

Canon Largo

CARSON NATIONAL FOREST

JICARILLA

APACHE

INDIAN

RESERVATION

Continental Divide

Navajo

Crownpoint

CHACO CULTURE N.H.P.

Gallup

Rio Grande

Chama

CARSON

Wheeler Peak 13,161 ft 4,011 m

NATIONAL

TAOS I.R.

Taos

Highest point in New Mexico

Sangre de Cristo Mts.

FOREST

SANTE FE

Chimayo

SANTA CLARA I.R.

Los Alamos

NAT.

BANDELIER N.M.

NAMBE I.R.

Pecos Baldy Lake

Santa Fe

Las Vegas

JEMEZ IND. RES.

ZIA IND. RES.

COCHITI I.R.

SANTO DOMINGO I.R.

SANTA ANA I.R.

SAN FELIPE I.R.

FOREST

LAS VEGAS N.W.R.

Gallinas

ZUNI

INDIAN

RES.

Zuni

Zuni

RAMAH NAVAJO IND. RES.

Milan

Grants

Rio San Jose

EL MALPAIS N.M.

ACOMA I.R.

CIBOLA NATIONAL FOREST

TO'HAJIILEE NAVAJO I.R.

LAGUNA I.R.

SANDIA I.R.

Bernalillo

Rio Rancho

Albuquerque

CIBOLA

Moriarty

LAGUNA INDIAN RESERVATION

ISLETA IND. RES.

ALAMO NAVAJO I.R.

Los Lunas

Belen

NATIONAL

Estancia

Rio Puerco

SEVILLETA N.W.R.

Mountainair

FOREST

Raton

Dry Cimarron

MAXWELL N.W.R.

Corrumpa Creek

Carrizo Creek

Clayton

Springer

Canadian

KIOWA AND RITA BLANCA

NATIONAL GRASSLANDS

Mora

Ute Creek

Conchas Lake

Conchas

Canadian

Tucumcari

Santa Rosa Lake

Santa Rosa

Pecos

OKLA.

N E W   M E X I C O

CIBOLA

NATIONAL

FOREST

Reserve

San Francisco

GILA

NATIONAL

FOREST

Black Range

Silver City

Bayard

Gila

Lordsburg

Deming

Socorro

BOSQUE DEL APACHE N.W.R.

Elephant Butte Res.

Truth or Consequences

Caballo Reservoir

Continental Divide

San Andres Mountains

Carrizozo

Sacramento Mountains

Gallo Arroyo

Arroyo del Macho

LINCOLN

MESCALERO APACHE INDIAN RES.

Tularosa

Alamogordo

WHITE SANDS N.M.

SAN ANDRES N.W.R.

Las Cruces

Anthony

NATIONAL

FOREST

Sumner Lake

Fort Sumner

Pecos

R   O   C   K   Y   M   O   U   N   T   A   I   N   S

Rio Hondo

Roswell

BITTER LAKE N.W.R.

Hagerman

Artesia

Rio Peñasco

Brantley Lake

Guadalupe Mts

FOREST

Carlsbad

Loving

CARLSBAD CAVERNS N.P.

Pecos

Clovis

Portales

L L A N O

E S T A C A D O

Lovington

Hobbs

Eunice

T E X A S

U.S.

MEXICO

MEXICO

FOREST

CORONADO NATIONAL FOREST

U.S.

MEXICO

SONORA

Sunland Park

Rio Grande

U.S. MEXICO

CHIHUAHUA

0   50 miles

0   75 kilometers

N

Map Key

★ State capital

••• City or town

.... Boundary

Indian Reservation

National Monument National Park

National Forest

National Wildlife Refuge

The Southwest

Oklahoma

 Land & Water Black Mesa, the Wichita Mountains, and the Arkansas River are important land and water features of Oklahoma.

 Statehood Oklahoma became the 46th state in 1907.

 People & Places Oklahoma's population is 3,642,361. Oklahoma City is the state capital and the largest city.

 Fun Fact Before it became a state, Oklahoma was known as Indian Territory. Today 39 Indian nations, including Cherokees, Osages, Creeks, and Choctaws, have their headquarters in the state.

▲ A tornado is a destructive rotating column of air that forms from a thunderstorm. In 1974, five tornadoes struck **Oklahoma City** in one day.

Oklahoma State Flag

Mistletoe State Flower

Scissor-Tailed Flycatcher State Bird

▲ The Golden Driller, with his hand on an oil rig, stands 76 feet (23 m) tall near the State Fairgrounds in **Tulsa**.

KANSAS

MISSOURI

Buffalo
Alva
SALT PLAINS N.W.R.
Great Salt Plains Lake
Salt Fork
Blackwell
Chikaskia
Ponca City
Kaw Lake
OSAGE NATION
INDIAN
Pawhuska
Arkansas
Caney
Neosho
Miami
Lake O' The Cherokees
Bartlesville
Vinita
Grove
Verdigris

Woodward
Fairview
Enid
Perry
Rock Creek
Sooner Lake
Keystone Lake
Skiatook Lake
RES.
Owasso
Oologah Lake
Pryor
Lake Hudson
Claremore

Wolf Creek
North Canadian
Cimarron
Stillwater
Sand Springs
Tulsa
Ft. Gibson Lake
Illinois

OKLAHOMA
Kingfisher
Guthrie
Cushing
Bristow
Broken Arrow
Sapulpa
Bixby
Tahlequah
Tenkiller Lake
Sallisaw

BLACK KETTLE NATIONAL GRASSLAND
WASHITA N.W.R.
Clinton
El Reno
Yukon
Edmond
Oklahoma City
Bethany
Deep Fork
Muskogee
Okmulgee
Henryetta
Arkansas
SEQUOYAH N.W.R.

Sayre
Elk City
Washita
Moore
Shawnee
Norman
Seminole
N. Canadian
Robert S. Kerr Lake
Poteau

North Fork
Hobart
Anadarko
Chickasha
Purcell
Little
Holdenville
Eufaula Lake
Canadian
McAlester
Heavener

Elm Fork
Lake Altus
Mangum
Wichita Mts.
Ada
Pauls Valley
Sardis Lake
OUACHITA

Hollis
Salt Fork
Altus
WICHITA MTS. WILDLIFE REFUGE
Lawton
Marlow
Duncan
Sulphur
CHICKASAW N.R.A.
McGee Cr. Lake
Atoka
Kiamichi
Ouachita Mountains
NATIONAL

Frederick
Walters
Waurika Lake
Arbuckle Mts.
Washita
TISHOMINGO N.W.R.
Muddy Boggy Cr.
Antlers
Little
Broken Bow Lake
Mountain Fork

Prairie Dog Town Fork
Red
Ardmore
Lake Texoma
Blue
Hugo
Hugo Lake
Idabel
FOREST

TEXAS
Red
Durant
Red

OZARK PLATEAU
ARKANSAS

0 ——— 50 miles
0 ——— 75 kilometers
N

Map Key

★ State capital
• • • City or town
...... Boundary

	Indian Reservation
	National Recreation Area
	National Forest
	National Grassland
	National Wildlife Refuge

◀ Young girls dressed in traditional costumes reflect the strong Native American heritage in **Oklahoma.**

▶ The collared lizard is Oklahoma's state reptile. The lizard is found in the Wichita Mountains and throughout the state.

The Southwest

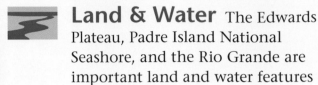

Texas

▲ The brightly lit Congress Avenue Bridge crosses the Town Lake, leading into downtown **Austin** where tall buildings rise against the night sky.

Land & Water The Edwards Plateau, Padre Island National Seashore, and the Rio Grande are important land and water features of Texas.

Statehood Texas became the 28th state in 1845.

People & Places The population of Texas is 24,326,974. Austin is the state capital. The largest city is Houston.

Fun Fact Over the course of its history, six different national flags have flown over Texas—Spanish, French, Mexican, Texan, Confederate, and American.

NEW MEXICO

U.S. ● El Paso
MEXICO

GUADALUPE MTS. N.P.

R O C K Y

+ *Guadalupe Peak*
8,749 ft
2,667 m

Highest point in Texas

CHIHUAHUA

Rio Grande

Davis Mts

Marfa ● M

Presidio ●

◄ Texas leads the U.S. in oil and natural gas production. A well near **Houston** pumps oil, called "black gold" because it's worth so much money.

Texas State Flag

▼ The colorful coach whip snake is found in **west Texas**. It can grow up to 6 feet (1.8 m) in length.

Mockingbird State Bird

Bluebonnet State Flower

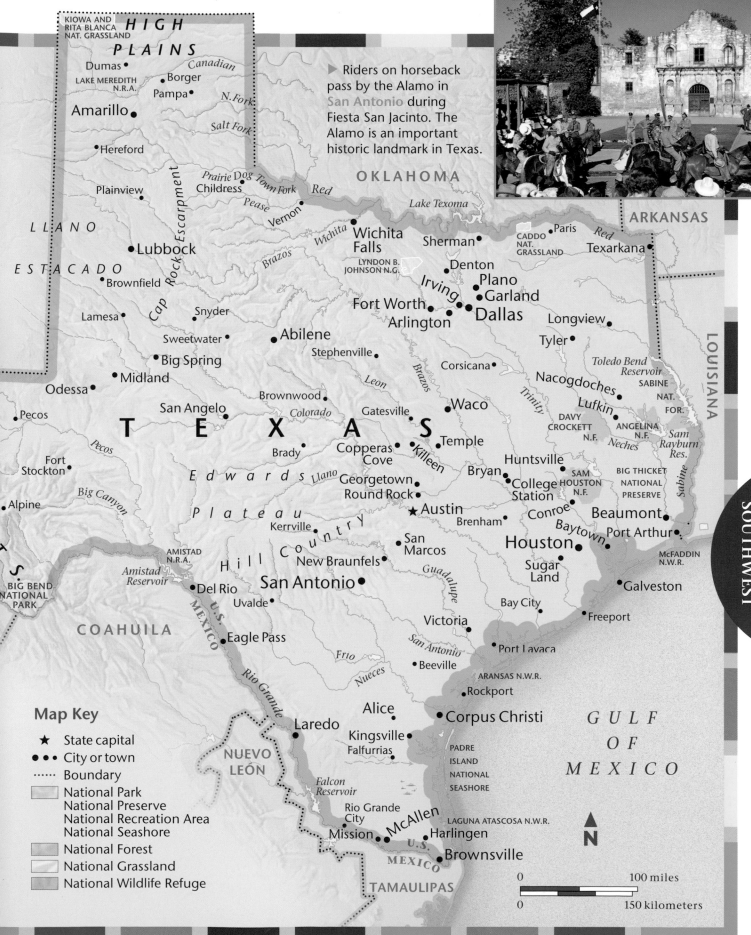

HIGH PLAINS

KIOWA AND RITA BLANCA NAT. GRASSLAND

Dumas

Borger
Pampa
LAKE MEREDITH N.R.A.

Amarillo

Canadian

N. Fork

Salt Fork

Hereford

Plainview

LLANO

Childress

Prairie Dog Town Fork

Pease

Vernon

Red

ESTACADO

Lubbock

Brownfield

Cap Rock Escarpment

Brazos

Wichita

Wichita Falls

LYNDON B. JOHNSON N.G.

Sherman

Lake Texoma

CADDO NAT. GRASSLAND

Paris

Red

Texarkana

OKLAHOMA

ARKANSAS

Riders on horseback pass by the Alamo in *San Antonio* during Fiesta San Jacinto. The Alamo is an important historic landmark in Texas.

Lamesa

Snyder

Sweetwater

Big Spring

Midland

Odessa

Pecos

Pecos

Fort Stockton

Big Canyon

Alpine

San Angelo

Abilene

Stephenville

Colorado

Leon

Brownwood

Gatesville

Brazos

Denton

Irving
Plano
Fort Worth
Garland
Arlington
Dallas

Longview

Tyler

Corsicana

Trinity

Waco

Temple

Nacogdoches

Lufkin

Toledo Bend Reservoir

SABINE NAT. FOR.

DAVY CROCKETT N.F.

ANGELINA N.F.

Neches

Sam Rayburn Res.

LOUISIANA

T E X A S

Brady

Copperas Cove

Killeen

Huntsville

Bryan

College Station

SAM HOUSTON N.F.

BIG THICKET NATIONAL PRESERVE

Sabine

Edwards

Llano

Georgetown

Round Rock

★ Austin

Conroe

Baytown

Beaumont

Port Arthur

Plateau

Kerrville

Country

New Braunfels

Brenham

San Marcos

Houston

Sugar Land

McFADDIN N.W.R.

Hill

AMISTAD N.R.A.

Amistad Reservoir

Del Rio

San Antonio

Guadalupe

Bay City

Galveston

Freeport

BIG BEND NATIONAL PARK

Uvalde

Eagle Pass

Frio

Nueces

San Antonio

Victoria

Port Lavaca

ARANSAS N.W.R.

Rockport

COAHUILA

Rio Grande

U.S.

MEXICO

Alice

Laredo

Kingsville

Falfurrias

Corpus Christi

*G U L F
O F
M E X I C O*

NUEVO LEÓN

Falcon Reservoir

Rio Grande City

Mission

McAllen

Harlingen

U.S.

MEXICO

Brownsville

PADRE ISLAND NATIONAL SEASHORE

Beeville

LAGUNA ATASCOSA N.W.R.

TAMAULIPAS

Map Key

★ State capital

••• City or town

···· Boundary

National Park
National Preserve
National Recreation Area
National Seashore

National Forest

National Grassland

National Wildlife Refuge

N

0   100 miles

0   150 kilometers

THE SOUTHWEST

The West

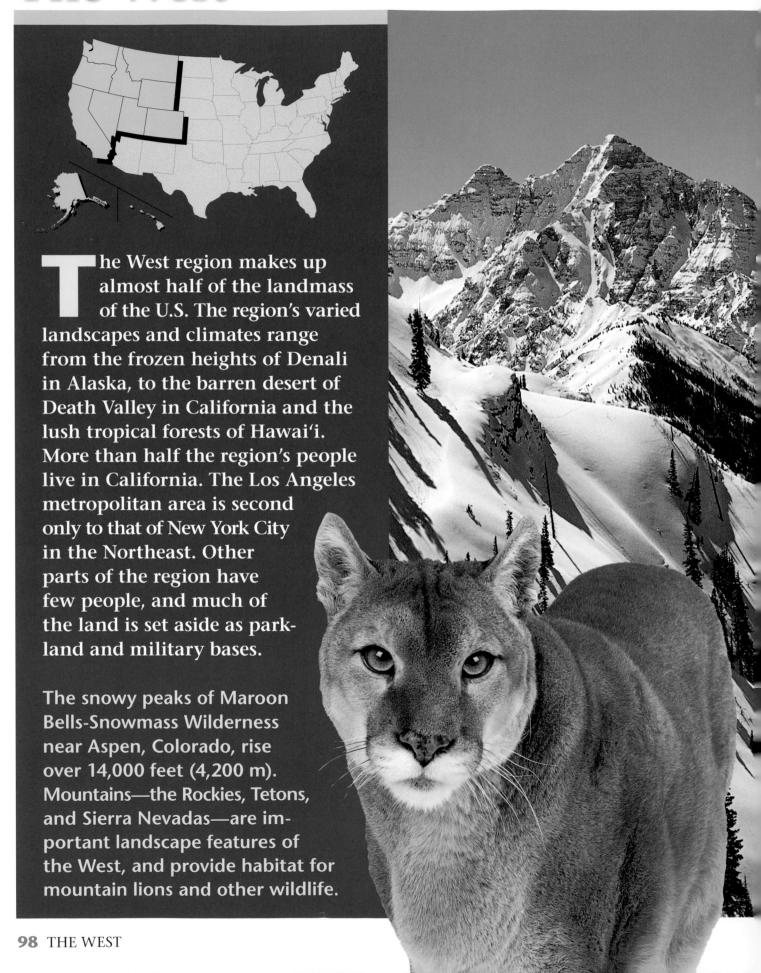

The West region makes up almost half of the landmass of the U.S. The region's varied landscapes and climates range from the frozen heights of Denali in Alaska, to the barren desert of Death Valley in California and the lush tropical forests of Hawai'i. More than half the region's people live in California. The Los Angeles metropolitan area is second only to that of New York City in the Northeast. Other parts of the region have few people, and much of the land is set aside as park-land and military bases.

The snowy peaks of Maroon Bells-Snowmass Wilderness near Aspen, Colorado, rise over 14,000 feet (4,200 m). Mountains—the Rockies, Tetons, and Sierra Nevadas—are im-portant landscape features of the West, and provide habitat for mountain lions and other wildlife.

Alaska

Land & Water The Tongass National Forest, Alaska Range, and the Yukon River are important land and water features of Alaska.

Statehood Alaska became the 49th state in 1959.

People & Places Alaska's population is 686,293. Juneau is the state capital. The largest city is Anchorage.

Fun Fact The most powerful earthquake ever recorded in North America struck Anchorage in 1964. Eighty times more powerful than the 1906 San Francisco earthquake, it measured 9.2 on the Richter scale.

Alaska State Flag

Forget-Me-Not State Flower

Willow Ptarmigan State Bird

▲ Dog sledding has a long and colorful history in Alaska. The most famous race is the Iditarod, which runs from Anchorage to **Nome** along an old mail and supply route.

CHUKCHI

RUSSIA

Bering

St. Lawrence I.

St. Matthew I.
ALASKA MARITIME N.W.R.

Nunivak I.

B E R I N G

St. Paul S E A

• Pribilof Islands
ALASKA MARITIME N.W.R.

◄ Native peoples in Alaska carved totem poles to tell their history. Carvers still make totem poles at Saxman Native Village in **Ketchikan**.

A L E U T I A N   I S L A N D S
Unimak I.
Unalaska I.
Umnak I. •Unalaska
ALASKA MARITIME NATIONA
Islands of Four Mountains
Yunaska I.

P A C I F I C
O C E A N

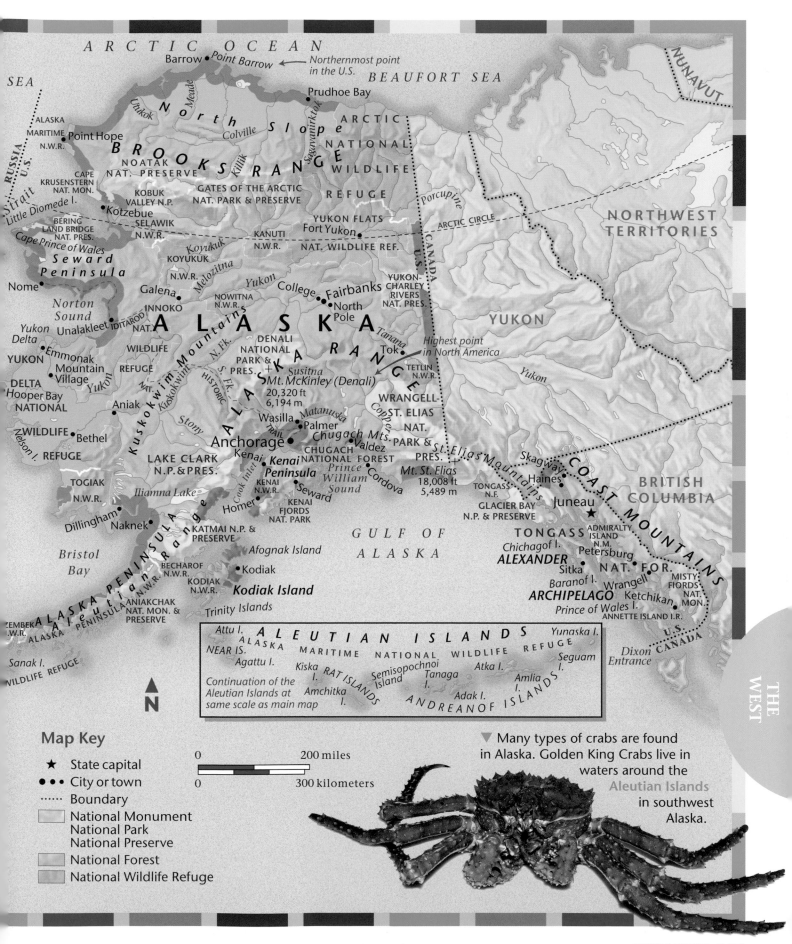

ARCTIC OCEAN

Barrow • Point Barrow ← Northernmost point
in the U.S.

BEAUFORT SEA

SEA

RUSSIA
U.S.

Little Diomede I.

ALASKA
MARITIME
N.W.R. • Point Hope

Strait

CAPE
KRUSENSTERN
NAT. MON.

Cape Prince of Wales

• Kotzebue

NOATAK
NAT. PRESERVE

KOBUK
VALLEY N.P.

GATES OF THE ARCTIC
NAT. PARK & PRESERVE

North Slope

B R O O K S   R A N G E

Meade

Unkok

Colville

Killik

Sagavanirktok

ARCTIC

NATIONAL

WILDLIFE

REFUGE

Porcupine

ARCTIC CIRCLE

NUNAVUT

**NORTHWEST
TERRITORIES**

BERING
LAND BRIDGE
NAT. PRES.

SELAWIK
N.W.R.

KANUTI
N.W.R.

YUKON FLATS
Fort Yukon

NAT. WILDLIFE REF.

*Seward
Peninsula*

Nome •

*Norton
Sound*

Galena •

KOYUKUK
N.W.R.

Koyukuk

NOWITNA
N.W.R.

INNOKO
NAT.

Melozitna

Yukon

College • Fairbanks
• North
Pole

YUKON-
CHARLEY
RIVERS
NAT. PRES.

U.S.
CANADA

YUKON

*Yukon
Delta*

Unalakleet • IDITAROD

A L A S K A

WILDLIFE

A L A S K A   R A N G E

Tanana Tok •

TETLIN
N.W.R.

Yukon

YUKON
DELTA

Emmonak •
Mountain
Village

REFUGE

NAT.

DENALI
NATIONAL
PARK &
PRES.

Susitna

Mt. McKinley (Denali)
20,320 ft
6,194 m

Highest point
in North America

Hooper Bay
NATIONAL

Aniak •

Stony

Kuskokwim Mountains

HISTORIC

S. Fk.

N. Fk.

Matanuska

Wasilla •
• Palmer

**WRANGELL-
ST. ELIAS
NAT.**

Copper

St. Elias Mountains

Skagway •

COAST MOUNTAINS

**BRITISH
COLUMBIA**

Z**WILDLIFE** • Bethel

Nelson I.

REFUGE

Anchorage

CHUGACH
NATIONAL
FOREST

Chugach Mts.

• Valdez

**PARK &
PRES.**

Mt. St. Elias
18,008 ft
5,489 m

TOGIAK
N.W.R.

Iliamna Lake

LAKE CLARK
N.P. & PRES.

Kenai

*Kenai
Peninsula*

Kenai

Cook Inlet

KENAI
N.W.R.

• Cordova

Haines •

TONGASS
N.F.

Juneau ★

TONGASS

Petersburg •

NAT. FOR.

Dillingham •

Naknek •

BECHAROF
N.W.R.

• Seward

KENAI
FJORDS
NAT. PARK

*Prince
William
Sound*

GLACIER BAY
N.P. & PRESERVE

ADMIRALTY
ISLAND
N.M.

Chichagof I.

ALEXANDER

Sitka •

MISTY
FIORDS
NAT.
MON.

*Bristol
Bay*

A L A S K A   P E N I N S U L A

Aleutian Range

KATMAI N.P. &
PRESERVE

Homer •

• Kodiak

Afognak Island

KODIAK
N.W.R.

Kodiak Island

Trinity Islands

**GULF OF
ALASKA**

Baranof I. • Wrangell

ARCHIPELAGO Ketchikan •

Prince of Wales I.

ANNETTE ISLAND I.R.

ANIAKCHAK
NAT. MON. &
PRESERVE

ZEMBEK
N.W.R.

ALASKA
PENINSULA

Sanak I.
WILDLIFE REFUGE

Attu I. **A L E U T I A N   I S L A N D S**

Yunaska I.

ALASKA

MARITIME   NATIONAL   WILDLIFE   REFUGE

NEAR IS.

Agattu I.

*Kiska
I.* RAT ISLANDS

*Semisopochnoi
Island*

*Tanaga
I.*

Atka I.

*Seguam
I.*

U.S.

*Dixon
Entrance*

CANADA

*Continuation of the
Aleutian Islands at
same scale as main map*

*Amchitka
I.*

Adak I.

*Amlia
I.*

A N D R E A N O F   I S L A N D S

N

Map Key

★ State capital

• • • City or town

• • • • Boundary

National Monument
National Park
National Preserve

National Forest

National Wildlife Refuge

0   200 miles
0   300 kilometers

▼ Many types of crabs are found
in Alaska. Golden King Crabs live in
waters around the
Aleutian Islands
in southwest
Alaska.

**THE
WEST**

California

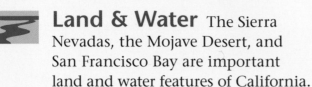

![Land & Water icon] **Land & Water** The Sierra Nevadas, the Mojave Desert, and San Francisco Bay are important land and water features of California.

![Statehood icon] **Statehood** California became the 31st state in 1850.

![People & Places icon] **People & Places** California's population is 36,756,666. Sacramento is the state capital. The largest city is Los Angeles.

![Fun Fact icon] **Fun Fact** Death Valley is the hottest place in the U.S. In July 1913, what is now Furnace Creek Ranch registered a temperature of 134°F (57°C).

▶ Stretching more than a mile (1.6 km) across the entrance to **San Francisco Bay**, the Golden Gate Bridge opened in 1937.

▲ An elephant seal on one of California's **Channel Islands** roars at a photographer who has invaded the seal's territory on the beach.

▼ Automobiles can drive through the base of this California redwood tree in **Leggett**, nicknamed the "Chandelier Tree" because of its huge branches.

![California State Flag]

CALIFORNIA REPUBLIC

California State Flag

Golden Poppy State Flower

California Quail State Bird

Chandelier Tree
Height 315 ft. Diameter 21 ft.
Maximum Age 2400 yrs.
DRIVE-THRU TREE PARK, Leggett CA

OREGON
IDAHO

SISKIYOU N.F.
ROGUE RIVER NAT. FOR.
LOWER KLAMATH N.W.R.
TULE LAKE N.W.R.
Goose Lake

Crescent City
SIX
Klamath
Yreka
LAVA BEDS N.M.
MODOC

REDWOOD NATIONAL PARK
KLAMATH NAT. FOR.
CASCADE RANGE
Alturas
NATIONAL

HOOPA VALLEY I.R.
SHASTA-WHISKEYTOWN-SHASTA-TRINITY N.R.A.
Shasta Lake
FOREST

Eureka
TRINITY
NAT.
Redding
FOREST
Eagle Lake

LASSEN NATIONAL
Susanville
Honey Lake

Leggett
MENDOCINO
NAT.
PLUMAS NAT. FOREST

ROUND VALLEY I.R.
NAT. FOR.
Chico
SIERRA

Fort Bragg
SACRAMENTO N.W.R.
Yuba City
TAHOE NAT. FOREST

Ukiah
Clear Lake
Lake Tahoe

Point Arena
ELDORADO NAT. FOR.
TOIYABE

Santa Rosa
Sacramento ★
STANISLAUS NAT. FOR.
NATIONAL FOR.

POINT REYES NATIONAL SEASHORE
San Rafael
Vallejo
Stockton
Mono Lake

San Francisco
Berkeley
Oakland
YOSEMITE NATIONAL PARK
INYO

Palo Alto
Modesto
NEVADA

San Jose
Merced
SIERRA NAT.
NATIONAL

Santa Cruz
Castroville
Bishop
FOREST

Monterey Bay
Salinas
KINGS CANYON NAT. PARK
DEATH VALLEY
MOJAVE

Monterey
PINNACLES N.M.
Fresno
NATIONAL
Highest point in the 48 contiguous U.S.

PACIFIC
OCEAN
LOS PADRES NAT. FOR.
Hanford
Visalia
Mt. Whitney 14,494 ft 4,418 m
Lowest point in North America; highest recorded temperature in the U.S., 134°F (57°C)

Tulare
SEQUOIA N.P.
SEQUOIA
VALLEY

Paso Robles
Atascadero
San Joaquin
Delano
TULE RIVER I.R.
NAT.
-282 ft -86 m
PARK

San Luis Obispo
KERN N.W.R.
FOREST
Ridgecrest
DESERT

Santa Maria
Bakersfield
MOJAVE NAT. PRESERVE
FORT MOJAVE I.R.

Lompoc
CARRIZO PLAIN N.M.
LOS PADRES
Barstow
Colorado

Santa Barbara
NAT. FOR.
ANGELES
Lancaster
Needles
Lake Havasu
CHEMEHUEVI I.R.

CHANNEL ISLANDS NATIONAL PARK
Ventura
Oxnard
SANTA MONICA MTS. N.R.A.
Simi Valley
NAT. FOR.
Pasadena
San Bernardino
Palm Springs
COLORADO RIVER I.R.

Santa Cruz
Santa Monica
Los Angeles
Anaheim
SAN BERNARDINO NAT. FOR.
JOSHUA TREE NAT. PARK
SONORAN

Santa Rosa
Long Beach
Santa Ana
Riverside
AGUA CALIENTE I.R.
SANTA ROSA & SAN JACINTO MTS. N.M.
Blythe

Santa Catalina
CLEVELAND NAT.
PALA I.R.
LOS COYOTES I.R.
Salton Sea

CHANNEL ISLANDS
Oceanside
FOR.
DESERT

San Clemente
Escondido
CAPITAN GRANDE I.R.
El Centro
Imperial Valley
IMPERIAL N.W.R.

San Diego
Calexico
FORT YUMA I.R.
Colorado

Chula Vista
U.S.
MEXICO

BAJA CALIFORNIA
SONORA

California produces almost all the artichokes grown in the U.S. Castroville claims the title "Artichoke Center of the World."

UTAH
NEVADA
ARIZONA

Map Key

★ State capital
••• City or town
····· Boundary
Indian Reservation
National Monument
National Park
National Preserve
National Recreation Area
National Forest
National Wildlife Refuge

0 —— 100 miles
0 —— 150 kilometers

N

The West

Colorado

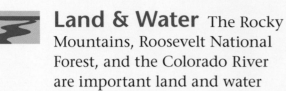

Land & Water The Rocky Mountains, Roosevelt National Forest, and the Colorado River are important land and water features of Colorado.

Statehood Colorado became the 38th state in 1876.

People & Places Colorado's population is 4,939,456. Denver is the state capital and the largest city.

Fun Fact The 700-foot- (210-m-) high sand dunes in Great Sand Dunes National Park occupy an area that was covered by an ancient sea more than one million years ago.

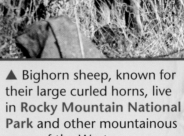

▲ Bighorn sheep, known for their large curled horns, live in **Rocky Mountain National Park** and other mountainous areas of the West.

▼ Early native people built more than 600 stone structures on protected cliffs of the canyon walls in **Mesa Verde National Park.**

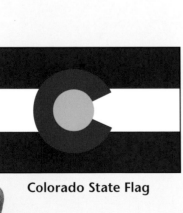

Colorado State Flag

Columbine State Flower

Lark Bunting State Bird

BROWNS PARK N.W.R.

Green

Vermillion Cr.

DINOSAUR NATIONAL MONUMENT

Little

Danforth

Rangely

White

Cathedral Bluffs

Roan Plateau

UTAH

Grand Valley

Grand Junction

Colorado

COLORADO NAT. MON.

Grand

GRAND MESA N.F.

Uncompahgre

Dolores

MANTI-LA SAL N.F.

UNCOMPAHGRE Plateau

San Miguel

NATIONAL

SAN

CANYONS OF THE ANCIENTS N.M.

Cortez

MESA VERDE N.P.

FOUR CORNERS

San Juan

UTE MOUNTAIN I.R.

Mancos

ARIZONA

Only spot in the U.S. where the borders of 4 states come together

Map of Colorado

WYOMING

NEBRASKA

Snake

Elkhead Mts.

ROUTT

North Platte

Medicine Bow Mts.

Laramie Mts.

ROOSEVELT

Hereford

North Sterling Reservoir

PAWNEE NATIONAL GRASSLAND

Sterling

Frenchman Creek

Holyoke

Craig

Steamboat Springs

ARAPAHO N.W.R.

NATIONAL

Continental

Park Range

Fort Collins

ROCKY

Greeley

Yampa

Divide

MOUNTAIN

NATIONAL

Loveland

South Platte

Fort Morgan

Akron

Hills

Colorado

NAT.

ROCKY MOUNTAIN NAT. PARK

Estes Park

Longmont

Gore Range

Meeker

FOREST

ARAPAHO

FOREST

Boulder

Brighton

Last Chance

WHITE

ARAPAHO N.R.A.

NATIONAL

Thornton

White River Plateau

Blue

Westminster

★ **Denver**

Arikaree

South Fork Republican

RIVER

Colorado

Glenwood Springs

FOREST

Arvada

Aurora

Rifle

Carbondale

Vail

Littleton

Castle Rock

Limon

Burlington

NATIONAL

FOREST

PIKE

Rampart Range

Big Sandy Creek

GRAND MESA NAT. FOR.

Aspen

Leadville

NATIONAL

Mesa

Highest point in Colorado

+ Mt. Elbert 14,433 ft 4,399 m

Range

Cheyenne Wells

GUNNISON

COLORADO

FOREST

Rush Creek

Delta

BLACK CANYON OF THE GUNNISON N.P.

SAN

Colorado Springs

Great Plains Reservoirs

NATIONAL

Gunnison

Salida

Arkansas

Fountain

Uncompahgre

CURECANTI N.R.A.

Blue Mesa Reservoir

Cañon City

Lake Meredith

Montrose

FOREST

ISABEL

Wet Mountains

John Martin Res.

Arkansas

RIO GRANDE

Sangre de

St. Charles

Rocky Ford

Las Animas

Lamar

FOREST

Telluride

Continental Divide

Saguache Cr.

San Luis

GREAT SAND DUNES N.P. & PRES.

NATIONAL

Pueblo

La Junta

SAN

Rio Grande

San Luis Valley

Cristo Mountains

Apishapa

COMANCHE

Two Butte Creek

Los Pinos

Piedra

JUAN

Pagosa Springs

MONTE VISTA N.W.R.

FOREST

San Luis Lake

Huerfano

Walsenburg

Bear Cr.

Springfield

NAT. FOREST

Durango

San Juan Mountains

Alamosa

ALAMOSA N.W.R.

FOREST

Culebra Ra.

Purgatoire

NATIONAL

Sand Arroyo

SOUTHERN UTE INDIAN RESERVATION

Conejos

Trinidad

Mesa de Maya

GRASSLAND

North Fork

NEW MEXICO

OKLAHOMA

Cimarron

Map Key

★ State capital

••• City or town

⋯⋯ Boundary

▧ Indian Reservation

▧ National Monument
National Park
National Preserve
National Recreation Area

▧ National Forest

▧ National Grassland

▧ National Wildlife Refuge

N

0 ___ 50 miles
0 ___ 75 kilometers

◀ An average annual snowfall of more than 130 inches (330 cm) attracts people who love winter sports to **Aspen**. This snowboarder maneuvers through tree-covered slopes.

The West

Hawai'i

Land & Water Kilauea crater, Diamond Head, and Pearl Harbor are important land and water features of Hawai'i.

Statehood Hawai'i became the 50th state in 1959.

People & Places Hawai'i's population is 1,288,198. Honolulu is the state capital and the largest city.

Fun Fact Hawai'i is the fastest growing state in the U.S.—not in people, but in land. Active volcanoes are constantly creating new land as lava continues to flow.

Hawai'i State Flag

Hibiscus State Flower

Hawaiian Goose (Nene) State Bird

◀ Pu'u 'O'o vent on **Kilauea crater** has added more than 568 acres (230 ha) of new land to Hawai'i.

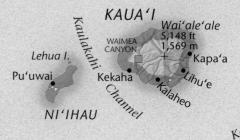

KAUA'I

Kaulakahi Channel

Lehua I.

Pu'uwai

NI'IHAU

WAIMEA CANYON

Wai'ale'ale 5,148 ft 1,569 m

Kekaha

Kalaheo

Lihu'e

Kapa'a

Kaua'i

▼ Hawai'i is the leading pineapple producer in the U.S. Pineapples are grown on Lana'i, Maui, and O'ahu.

PACIFIC

Kure Atoll

Midway Islands

Pearl and Hermes Atoll

Lisianski I.

Laysan I.

Maro Reef

NORTHWESTERN HAWAIIAN

0   200 miles

0   300 kilometers

N

◄ A surfer balances on his board. People travel great distances to ride the big waves off the North Shore of **O'ahu**.

► A young girl performs a traditional Polynesian hula on a misty day in Waimea Canyon on the island of Kaua'i.

► Green sea turtles migrate 800 miles (1,287 km) to their nesting area in the **Northwestern Hawaiian Islands**.

H A W A I I

Channel

O'AHU Kahuku Pt.
Waialua   La'ie
Ka'ena Pt.
Mililani Town Pearl City Kane'ohe
Waipahu   Kailua
Pearl Harbor   ★ Diamond Head
Honolulu   762 ft
                  232 m

Kaiwi Channel

KALAUPAPA N.H.P.   MOLOKA'I
              Waialua
Kaunakakai
          Lahaina   Kahului   MAUI
Lana'i City   Wailuku   Makawao
              Kihei
LANA'I   Pukalani
                      HALEAKALA N.P.

KAHO'OLAWE

O C E A N

'Alenuihaha Channel

Map Key
★ State capital
●●● City or town
▭ National Park

'Upolu Point
      Kapa'au
      Waimea (Kamuela)   Highest point in Hawai'i
Waikoloa
          Mauna Kea   HAKALAU FOREST N.W.R.
          13,796 ft
          4,205 m
Keahole Pt.
Kalaoa   Hilo
Kailua   Mauna Loa   • Mountain View
Holualoa 13,679 ft
          4,169 m
Captain Cook   Cape Kumukahi
              HAWAI'I   KILAUEA CRATER
              VOLCANOES
              NATIONAL   PARK   HAWAI'I
                    Pahala

Kalae (South Point)

Southernmost point in the U.S.

THE STATE OF HAWAI'I

The State of Hawai'i extends from the big island of Hawai'i to Kure Atoll. The 8 main islands are shown enlarged above.

Gardner Pinnacles

PACIFIC OCEAN

La Perouse Pinnacle   Necker I.
                Nihoa
              Kaua'i
I S L A N D S   O'ahu   Moloka'i
        Ni'ihau   Maui
        Honolulu ★ Lanai
              Kaho'olawe   Hilo
              Hawai'i

N

0   50 miles
0   75 kilometers

Idaho

Land & Water The Bitterroot Range, the Columbia Plateau, and the Snake River are important land and water features of Idaho.

Statehood Idaho became the 43rd state in 1890.

People & Places Idaho's population is 1,523,816. Boise is the state capital and the largest city.

Fun Fact In preparation for their mission to the moon, Apollo astronauts visited Craters of the Moon National Monument and Preserve to study its volcanic geology and experience its harsh environment.

Idaho State Flag

Syringa (Mock Orange) State Flower

Mountain Bluebird State Bird

▲ A wood duck perches on a post. These colorful waterfowl can be viewed in Kootenai National Wildlife Refuge near **Bonners Ferry.**

▲ More than 40 percent of Idaho's land area is forested. Use of this land is overseen by the Forest Products Commission in **Boise.** Forest products are important to the state's economy.

BRITISH COLUMBIA

ALBERTA

CANADA
U.S.

WASHINGTON

R O C K Y

KOOTENAI
N.W.R.
□ Bonners Ferry

KOOTENAI

Priest Lake

IDAHO

Selkirk Mts.

NATIONAL

Cabinet Mountains

FOREST

Pend Oreille

Priest

Kootenai

• Sandpoint

Clark Fork

PANHANDLE

Pend Oreille Lake

M O U N T A I N S

• Post Falls

Spokane •

Bitterroot Range

Coeur d'Alene

Coeur d'Alene Lake

Coeur d'Alene

• Kellogg

COEUR
D'ALENE
INDIAN
RES.

St. Joe

St. Maries

St. Maries •

NAT. FORESTS

▶ The moon rises over **Lemhi Pass.** Lewis and Clark crossed the Continental Divide here in 1805 on their journey west.

MONTANA

Moscow •

Dworshak Reservoir

N. Fk.

CLEARWATER

Lolo Pass

Potlatch

Orofino •

Clearwater

NAT.

FOREST

Clearwater

Lochsa

Clearwater

NEZ PERCE
INDIAN
RES.

Kamiah •

Selway

BITTERROOT

Shake

Lewiston •

Clearwater

• Grangeville

S. Fk.

Clearwater

NEZ PERCE
Mountains

NATIONAL

HELLS

Clearwater

NATIONAL FOREST

Nez Perce Pass

N

CANYON

Hells Canyon

Salmon

FOREST

Continental Divide

N.R.A.

• Riggins

PAYETTE

Salmon

Salmon •

Lemhi Fk.

Lemhi Pass

Henrys Lake

0   50 miles

0   75 kilometers

S. Fk.

Middle Fk.

NATIONAL   FOREST

CHALLIS

YELLOWSTONE

Brownlee Res.

McCall •

Salmon River

SALMON

Lemhi Range

Centennial Mts.

NATIONAL PARK

I D A H O
Mountains

Challis •

Lost River

Island Park Res.

Weiser

BOISE

Lost River Ra.

Highest point in Idaho

Snake

Cascade •

Salmon

Little Lost

TARGHEE   NATIONAL

WYOMING

Weiser •

Borah Peak
12,662 ft
3,859 m

Big Lost

CAMAS
N.W.R.

• St. Anthony

Payette •

NATIONAL

N. Fork

Sawtooth Ra.

SAWTOOTH

NAT. FOR.

F O R E S T

Mud Lake

• Rexburg

Snake

FOREST

Emmett •

Payette

S. Fork

N.R.A.

Smoky Mts.

Ketchum •

Arco •

Idaho Falls •

Rigby •

Caribou Ra.

Caldwell •

FOREST

★ Boise

Nampa •

Lake Lowell

DEER
FLAT N.W.R.

Anderson Ranch Res.

SAWTOOTH

Hailey •

Magic Res.

CRATERS
OF THE MOON
NAT. MON.
& PRES.

FORT HALL

Shelley •

Blackfoot •

CARIBOU

Palisades Res.

Grays Lake

GRAYS
LAKE
N.W.R.

Snake River Plain

Blackfoot Mts.

Blackfoot Res.

NATIONAL

OREGON

• Mountain Home

Gooding •

Big Wood

Little Wood

INDIAN
RES.

Chubbuck •

American
Falls •

Pocatello •

Bannock Ra.

Portneuf Ra.

• Soda
Springs

Owyhee Mts.

C.J. Strike
Reservoir

Glenns
Ferry •

Shoshone •

L. Walcott

Jerome •

FORT HALL

Rupert •

Bear

FOREST

Bear River Range

Battle Cr.

◀ About 60 percent of all potatoes grown in **Idaho** end up as French fries.

Jordan Cr.

Owyhee

Snake

Bruneau

HAGERMAN
FOSSIL BEDS
N.M.

Buhl •

Twin
Falls

Burley •

MINIDOKA
N.W.R.

Goose Cr.

Bannock Ra.

Malad
City •

CURLEW
NAT.
GRASSLAND

Montpelier •

BEAR LAKE
N.W.R.

S. Fk.

Owyhee

E. Fk. Bruneau

Jarbidge

SAWTOOTH   NAT. FOREST

Salmon Falls Cr. Res.

Preston •

Bear

Bear Lake

DUCK
VALLEY
INDIAN
RES.

Columbia Plateau

NEVADA

UTAH

Map Key

★ State capital

••• City or town

...... Boundary

▢ Indian Reservation

▢ National Park

▢ National Forest

▢ National Wildlife Refuge

Montana

Land & Water The Rocky Mountains, Great Plains, and the Yellowstone River are important land and water features of Montana.

Statehood Montana became the 41st state in 1889.

People & Places Montana's population is 967,440. Helena is the state capital. The largest city is Billings.

Fun Fact Montana is the only state with river systems that empty into the Gulf of Mexico to the southeast, Hudson Bay to the north, and the Pacific Ocean to the west.

Montana State Flag

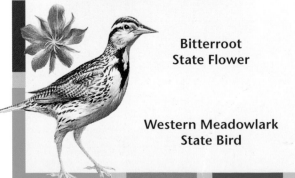

Bitterroot
State Flower

Western Meadowlark
State Bird

▲ Skiers ride a chairlift up a snowy mountain slope in **Whitefish**.

▼ Rugged peaks of the Northern Rocky Mountains are reflected in the still surface of a mountain lake in **Glacier National Park**.

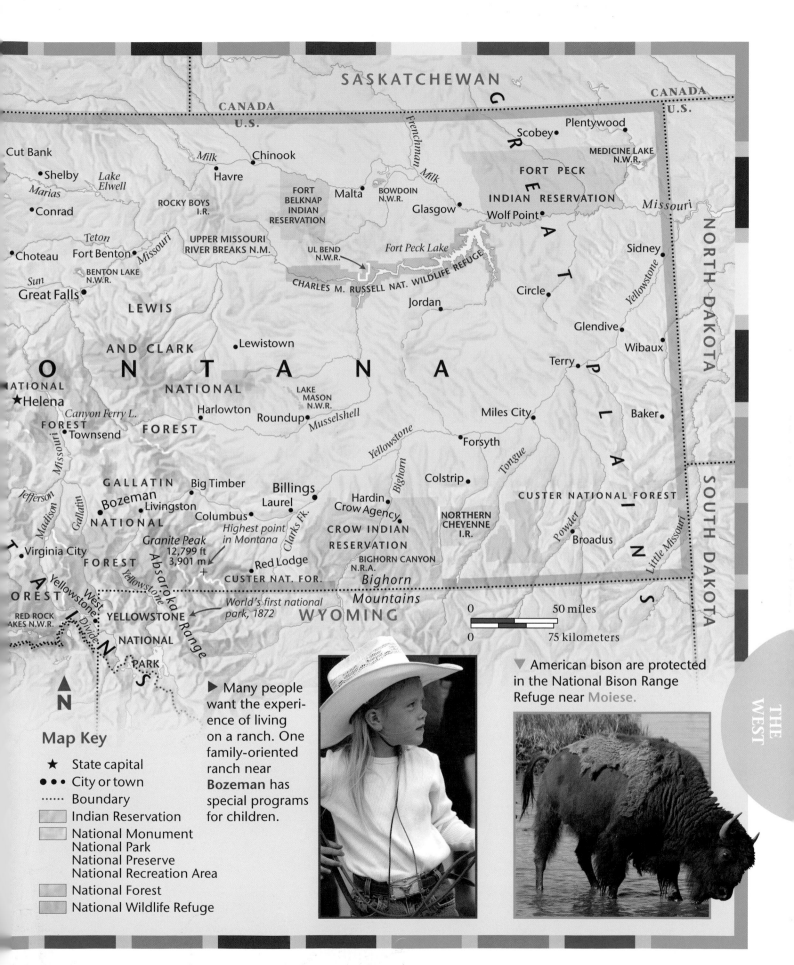

SASKATCHEWAN

CANADA
U.S.

CANADA
U.S.

Cut Bank

Shelby
Lake
Elwell
Marias

Conrad

Teton
Choteau   Fort Benton
BENTON LAKE
N.W.R.

Sun
Great Falls

ROCKY BOYS
I.R.

Milk   Chinook
Havre

FORT
BELKNAP
INDIAN
RESERVATION

Malta

UPPER MISSOURI
RIVER BREAKS N.M.

UL BEND
N.W.R.

Missouri

BOWDOIN
N.W.R.

Glasgow

Milk

Scobey
Plentywood

MEDICINE LAKE
N.W.R.

FORT PECK
INDIAN RESERVATION

Wolf Point

Frenchman

Fort Peck Lake

CHARLES M. RUSSELL NAT. WILDLIFE REFUGE

Jordan

Missouri

NORTH DAKOTA

Sidney

Circle

LEWIS

AND CLARK

Lewistown

NATIONAL

Missouri
★Helena

Canyon Ferry L.

FOREST
Townsend

FOREST

GALLATIN

Bozeman
Livingston

Jefferson

Madison
Virginia City

Gallatin

NATIONAL

FOREST

Big Timber

Columbus

Granite Peak
12,799 ft
3,901 m
+

Clarks Fk.

Red Lodge

CUSTER NAT. FOR.

Highest point
in Montana

Harlowton

LAKE
MASON
N.W.R.

Roundup

Musselshell

Billings

Laurel

Hardin
Crow Agency

CROW INDIAN
RESERVATION

BIGHORN CANYON
N.R.A.

Yellowstone

Forsyth

Colstrip

NORTHERN
CHEYENNE
I.R.

Bighorn

Tongue

Miles City

Glendive

Wibaux

Terry

Baker

CUSTER NATIONAL FOREST

Powder

Broadus

SOUTH DAKOTA

Little Missouri

Bighorn
Mountains

Absaroka Range

World's first national
park, 1872

WYOMING

RED ROCK
AKES N.W.R.

West
Yellowstone

Yellowstone

Divide

YELLOWSTONE

NATIONAL

PARK

N

0 _____ 50 miles
0 _____ 75 kilometers

▶ **Many people
want the experi-
ence of living
on a ranch. One
family-oriented
ranch near
Bozeman has
special programs
for children.**

▼ **American bison are protected
in the National Bison Range
Refuge near Moiese.**

Map Key

★ State capital
••• City or town
······ Boundary
▢ Indian Reservation
▢ National Monument
   National Park
   National Preserve
   National Recreation Area
▢ National Forest
▢ National Wildlife Refuge

Nevada

Land & Water The Great Basin, the Mojave Desert, and Lake Tahoe are important land and water features of Nevada.

Statehood Nevada became the 36th state in 1864.

People & Places Nevada's population is 2,600,167. Carson City is the state capital. The largest city is Las Vegas.

Fun Fact Between 1975 and 2000, the population of Clark County, home of Las Vegas, grew almost 250 percent. It is still one of the fastest-growing counties in the United States.

▲ The Luxor, recreating a scene from ancient Egypt, is one of many hotel-casinos that attract thousands of tourists to **Las Vegas.**

◄ Paiute Indians, dressed in traditional clothing, live on the Pyramid Lake Reservation near **Reno.** Their economy centers on fishing and recreational activities.

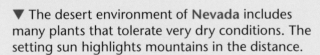

Nevada State Flag

▼ The desert environment of **Nevada** includes many plants that tolerate very dry conditions. The setting sun highlights mountains in the distance.

Mountain Bluebird State Bird

Sagebrush State Flower

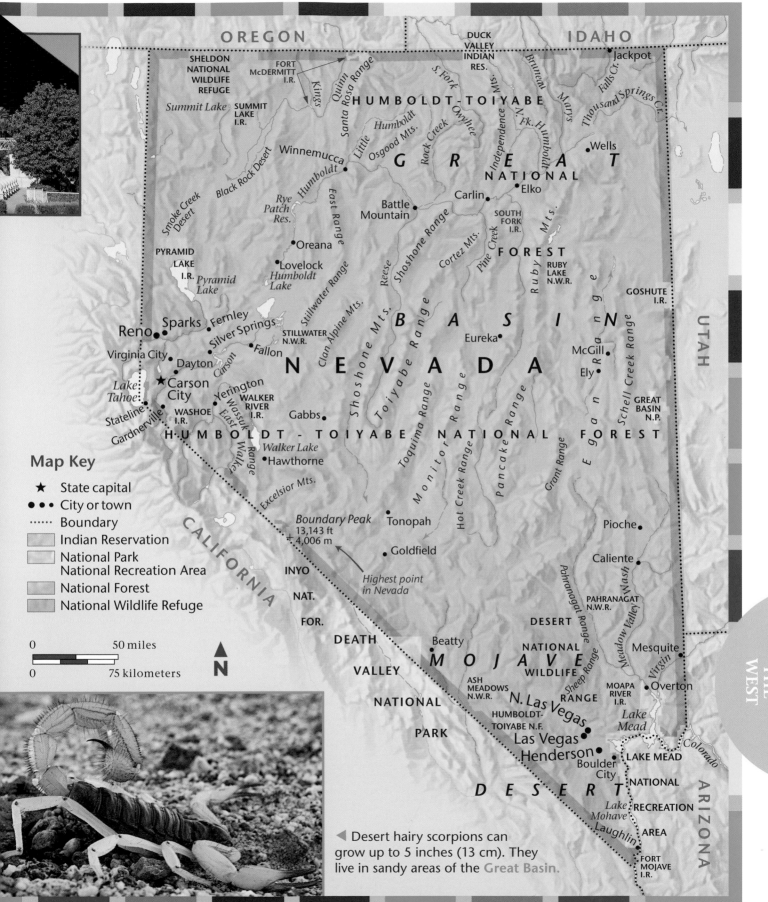

OREGON
IDAHO

DUCK
VALLEY
INDIAN
RES.

Jackpot

SHELDON
NATIONAL
WILDLIFE
REFUGE

FORT
McDERMITT
I.R.

Kings

Summit Lake

SUMMIT
LAKE
I.R.

Santa Rosa Range

Quinn River Range

HUMBOLDT-TOIYABE

S. Fork Owyhee

Bruneau

Mary's

Thousand Springs Cr.

Falls Cr.

Wells

Winnemucca

Little Humboldt

Humboldt

Osgood Mts.

Rock Creek

N. Fk. Humboldt

Independence Mts.

G R E A T

NATIONAL

Elko

Smoke Creek Desert

Black Rock Desert

Humboldt

Rye Patch Res.

East Range

Battle Mountain

Carlin

SOUTH FORK I.R.

Shoshone Range

Cortez Mts.

F O R E S T

Ruby Mts.

RUBY LAKE N.W.R.

GOSHUTE I.R.

PYRAMID LAKE I.R.

Pyramid Lake

Oreana

Lovelock

Humboldt Lake

Stillwater Range

Reese

Pine Creek

B A S I N

Ruby Range

Schell Creek Range

Sparks

Fernley

Silver Springs

STILLWATER N.W.R.

Clan Alpine Mts.

Shoshone Mts.

N E V A D A

Eureka

McGill

Reno

Virginia City

Dayton

Carson

Fallon

Ely

Lake Tahoe

Carson City

Yerington

WALKER RIVER I.R.

Gabbs

Toiyabe Range

Toquima Range

Monitor Range

Pancake Range

Grant Range

GREAT BASIN N.P.

Stateline

WASHOE I.R.

Wassuk Range

East Walker

Egan Range

Gardnerville

H U M B O L D T - T O I Y A B E   N A T I O N A L   F O R E S T

Walker Lake

Hawthorne

Excelsior Mts.

Hot Creek Range

Map Key

★ State capital
••• City or town
····· Boundary
  Indian Reservation
  National Park
  National Recreation Area
  National Forest
  National Wildlife Refuge

0 ──── 50 miles
0 ──── 75 kilometers

N

CALIFORNIA

Boundary Peak
13,143 ft
4,006 m

Tonopah

Goldfield

Highest point in Nevada

INYO

NAT.

FOR.

DEATH

VALLEY

NATIONAL

PARK

Beatty

ASH MEADOWS N.W.R.

M O J A V E

NATIONAL

WILDLIFE

RANGE

Pahranagat Range

Sheep Range

Pahranagat N.W.R.

Meadow Valley Wash

Pioche

Caliente

Mesquite

Virgin

MOAPA RIVER I.R.

Overton

DESERT

HUMBOLDT-TOIYABE N.F.

N. Las Vegas

Las Vegas

Henderson

Boulder City

LAKE MEAD

Lake Mead

Colorado

D E S E R T

NATIONAL

RECREATION

AREA

Lake Mohave

Laughlin

FORT MOJAVE I.R.

ARIZONA

UTAH

◄ Desert hairy scorpions can grow up to 5 inches (13 cm). They live in sandy areas of the Great Basin.

The West

Oregon

 Land & Water The Cascade Range, Crater Lake, and the Columbia River are important land and water features of Oregon.

 Statehood Oregon became the 33rd state in 1859.

 People & Places Oregon's population is 3,790,060. Salem is the state capital. The largest city is Portland.

 Fun Fact The Bonneville Power Administration, headquartered in Portland, provides about 45 percent of the electricity used in the Pacific Northwest. Most of this power comes from hydroelectric plants along the Columbia River.

Oregon State Flag

Oregon Grape
State Flower

Western Meadowlark
State Bird

▲ The 125-foot (38-m) Astoria Column near the mouth of the **Columbia River** is covered with scenes of historic events.

▲ The cool, moist climate of the valley of the Willamette River is well-suited to certain varieties of wine grapes.

▼ Rocky outcrops called sea stacks line Oregon's **Pacific coast**. They are remains of a former coastline that has been eroded by waves.

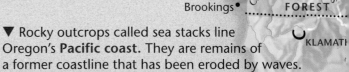

WASHINGTON

Columbia

Forest Grove
• St. Helens
Hillsboro •
Beaverton •
Portland • Gresham
MOUNT
Newburg •
Oregon City
• McMinnville
• Woodburn
BASKETT SLOUGH
N.W.R.
★ **Salem**
ANKENY
N.W.R.
• Albany
• Lebanon
Corvallis •
WILLAMETTE
McKenzie

HOOD

Mt. Hood
+11,239 ft 3,426 m

Hood
River • • The Dalles

COLUMBIA RIVER GORGE
NATIONAL SCENIC AREA

← Highest point
in Oregon

White

Deschutes

WARM
SPRINGS
INDIAN
RES.

• Madras

CROOKED RIVER
NATIONAL
GRASSLAND

DESCHUTES

John Day

Ochoco Mts.

OCHOCO

• Prineville

Hermiston •
• Pendleton

Heppner •

Columbia

Snake
Lake Wallula

Milton-Freewater •
COLD
SPRINGS
N.W.R.

UMATILLA

UMATILLA
INDIAN
RES.

NATIONAL

FOREST

MALHEUR

John Day •

NATIONAL

Grande Ronde

Snake

HELLS
CANYON

WALLOWA-
Wallowa
• Enterprise

WHITMAN

NATIONAL

RECREATION

AREA

• La Grande

NATIONAL

Powder

• Baker
City

*Brownlee
Res.*

IDAHO

B l u e   M o u n t a i n s

C O L U M B I A   P L A T E A U

C A S C A D E   R A N G E

PACIFIC CREST NATIONAL SCENIC TRAIL

FOREST

NAT.

Springfield
• Eugene

Cottage
Grove

UMPQUA

J. Umpqua

NATIONAL

FOREST

S. Umpqua

NATIONAL
FOREST

• Bend

NEWBERRY NATIONAL
VOLCANIC MONUMENT

High
Desert

Christmas
Lake
Valley

Crooked

Sycan

NATIONAL

FOREST

FOREST

Harney Basin

• Burns

Malheur

N. Fk.

Malheur

• Ontario

Malheur

Owyhee

Lake
Owyhee

• Redmond

O R E G O N

C A S C A D E

Rogue •
ROGUE

RIVER

• entral
Point
• Medford

Ashland •
FOREST

NAT.

CASCADE SISKIYOU
N.M.

Klamath
AT. FOR.

WINEMA FREMONT

Crater Lake ←
CRATER
LAKE N.P.

UPPER
KLAMATH
N.W.R.

Upper
Klamath
Lake

FOREST

← Deepest Lake in the U.S.,
1,932 ft 589 m

KLAMATH
FOREST
N.W.R.

Summer
Lake

NATIONAL

Sprague

Klamath Falls
• Altamont

Lakeview •

FOREST

Goose Lake

Harney
Lake

Malheur
Lake

MALHEUR
NATIONAL
WILDLIFE
REFUGE

*Lake
Abert*

HART MT.
NATIONAL
ANTELOPE
REFUGE

Warner Valley

G R E A T

Steens Mountain

FORT
McDERMITT
I.R.

Owyhee

Snake

CALIFORNIA

Map Key

★ State capital
• • • City or town
• • • • Boundary

Indian Reservation

National Monument
National Park
National Recreation Area
National Scenic Area

National Forest

National Wildlife Refuge

B A S I N

N

NEVADA

0   50 miles

0   75 kilometers

▶ The climate of
Oregon is ideal for
growing fir and spruce
Christmas trees.

The West

▲ Water sports such as inner tubing are popular activities in the **Glen Canyon National Recreation Area.**

Utah

Land & Water The Great Basin, the Uinta Mountains, and the Great Salt Lake are important land and water features of Utah.

Statehood Utah became the 45th state in 1896.

People & Places Utah's population is 2,736,424. Salt Lake City is the state capital and the largest city.

Fun Fact Great Salt Lake is the largest natural lake west of the Mississippi River. The lake, which has a high level of evaporation, is about eight times saltier than the ocean.

◀ A newly married couple stands in front of the Temple in Salt Lake City, where Mormons gather for religious ceremonies.

▼ **Arches National Park** includes more than 2,000 arches carved by natural forces over millions of years. Delicate Arch stands on the canyon edge, with the La Sal Mountains in the distance.

Utah State Flag

Sego Lilly

California Gull State Bird

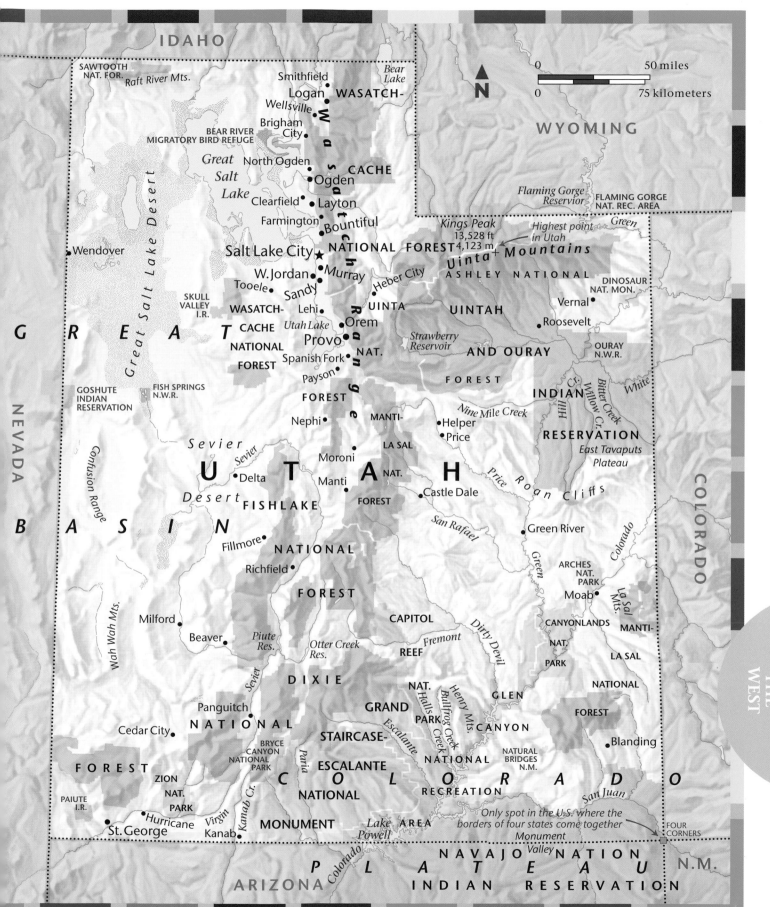

IDAHO

SAWTOOTH
NAT. FOR.   *Raft River Mts.*

Smithfield

*Bear
Lake*

WASATCH-

Logan

Wellsville

Brigham
City

CACHE

*Great
Salt
Lake*

North Ogden

Ogden

Clearfield   Layton

Wendover

Farmington

Bountiful

NATIONAL FOREST

Salt Lake City ★

W. Jordan   Murray

Tooele   Sandy

Heber City

WASATCH-

Lehi

UINTA

CACHE

Utah Lake

Orem

NATIONAL

Provo

NAT.

Spanish Fork

FOREST

Payson

SKULL
VALLEY
I.R.

GOSHUTE
INDIAN
RESERVATION

FISH SPRINGS
N.W.R.

Sevier

Nephi

FOREST

MANTI-

U   **T**   **A**   **H**

Sevier

Delta

Moroni

Manti

LA SAL

NAT.

Desert   **FISHLAKE**

FOREST

WYOMING

*Flaming Gorge
Reservoir*

FLAMING GORGE
NAT. REC. AREA

Green

Kings Peak
13,528 ft
4,123 m

Highest point
in Utah

Uinta ✛ *Mountains*

ASHLEY   NATIONAL

UINTAH

DINOSAUR
NAT. MON.

Vernal

Roosevelt

OURAY
N.W.R.

*Strawberry
Reservoir*

AND OURAY

FOREST

INDIAN

Hill Cr.

Willow Cr.

Bitter Creek

White

Nine Mile Creek

Helper

Price

RESERVATION

*East Tavaputs
Plateau*

G

R

E

A

T

Great Salt Lake Desert

NEVADA

B

A

S

I

N

Confusion Range

Wah Wah Mts.

Fillmore

Richfield

NATIONAL

FOREST

Milford

Beaver

*Piute
Res.*

*Otter Creek
Res.*

Sevier

DIXIE

Panguitch

NATIONAL

Cedar City

BRYCE
CANYON
NATIONAL
PARK

FOREST

ZION

PAIUTE
I.R.

NAT.

Hurricane

PARK

St. George

Kanab

Virgin

Kanab Cr.

Paria

MONUMENT

Castle Dale

San Rafael

Price

Roan Cliffs

Green River

Green

CAPITOL

REEF

Fremont

Dirty Devil

Colorado

ARCHES
NAT.
PARK

Moab

*La Sal
Mts.*

CANYONLANDS

NAT.

PARK

MANTI-

LA SAL

NATIONAL

NAT.

GRAND

STAIRCASE-

ESCALANTE

NATIONAL

MONUMENT

Escalante

Halls Creek

Bullfrog Creek

Henry Mts.

GLEN

CANYON

NATIONAL

RECREATION

AREA

NATURAL
BRIDGES
N.M.

FOREST

Blanding

San Juan

Only spot in the U.S. where the
borders of four states come together
Monument

*Lake
Powell*

Valley

C   **O**   **L**   **O**   **R**   **A**   **D**   **O**

COLORADO

FOUR
CORNERS

N.M.

ARIZONA

Colorado

P   **L**   **A**   **T**   **E**   **A**   **U**

NAVAJO

NATION

INDIAN   **RESERVATION**

0   50 miles

0   75 kilometers

N

Washington

 Land & Water

The Olympic Mountains, the Palouse Hills, and Puget Sound are important land and water features of Washington.

 Statehood Washington became the 42nd state in 1889.

People & Places

Washington's population is 6,549,224. Olympia is the state capital. The largest city is Seattle.

? Fun Fact Mt. Rainier, a dormant volcano, last erupted in 1969. Another nearby volcano, Mt. St. Helens, erupted in 1980. Ash from that eruption was carried by winds as far away as Maine.

▲ A Roosevelt elk grazes in the temperate rain forest of **Olympic National Forest**. Adult males weigh up to 1,000 pounds (454 kg).

◄ Seattle's modern skyline is easily recognized because of its Space Needle tower. The city is an important West Coast port.

Washington State Flag

Coast Rhododendron State Flower

American Goldfinch State Bird

Vancouver Island

PACIFIC OCEAN

Cape Flattery
MAKAH I.R.
Strait of Juan de Fuca
Port Angeles
Sol Duc
OLYMPIC N.F.
Olympic
OLYMPIC NAT. PAR
Mountain.
Queets
QUINAULT INDIAN RES.
FORES
Hoquiam
Aberdeen
Grays Harbor
Willapa Bay
Raymonc
WILLAPA N.W.R.
Cape Disappointment
Columbia
C O A S T   R A N G E S

0   50 miles
0   75 kilometers

Map Key

★   State capital
●●●   City or town
......   Boundary
  Indian Reservation
  National Monument
  National Park
  National Recreation Area
  National Scenic Area
  National Forest
  National Wildlife Refuge

CANADA
U.S.

CANADA
U.S. IDAHO

LUMMI
I.R.
Bellingham

NORTH
CASCADES
NATIONAL
PARK

Ross Lake

ROSS LAKE N.R.A.

OKANOGAN NATIONAL

FOREST

Okanogan

Republic

Columbia

RECREATION AREA

COLVILLE NATIONAL FOREST

PANHANDLE

Franklin
Delano
Roosevelt
Lake

Colville

LITTLE PEND OREILLE N.W.R.

NATIONAL

FORESTS

San Juan
Islands

Anacortes

Skagit

MOUNT

Omak

Methow

COLVILLE

Sampoil

KALISPELL
I.R.

Pend Oreille

Mount
Vernon

Oak Harbor

BAKER–

NATIONAL

SCENIC

LAKE CHELAN
N.R.A.

WENATCHEE

INDIAN

Colville

Whidbey
Island

Port
Townsend

TULALIP
I.R.

Everett

Lake
Chelan

RESERVATION

NATIONAL

SPOKANE
INDIAN
RES.

Opportunity

OLYMPIC

Kirkland

Skykomish

TRAIL

Columbia

LAKE

ROOSEVELT

Spokane

NAT.

SNOQUALMIE

Redmond

RANGE

NATIONAL

Grand Coulee

Banks
Lake

Spokane

Bremerton

Seattle

Bellevue

Puget Sound

FOREST

Columbia

Medical
Lake

TURNBULL
N.W.R.

PUYALLUP I.R.

Renton

Auburn

NAT.

W A S H I N G T O N

Shelton

Tacoma

CREST

Wenatchee

Ephrata

Moses Lake

Ritzville

Palouse

Puyallup

PACIFIC

Yakima

Potholes
Reservoir

Hills

Olympia

Mt. Rainier
14,411 ft
4,392 m

FOREST

Highest
point in
Washington

Ellensburg

Naches

COLUMBIA
N.W.R.

Othello

Pullman

Tumwater

Alder
Lake

MT. RAINIER
N.P.

SADDLE MT.
N.W.R.

Palouse

Centralia

MOUNT BAKER–
SNOQUALMIE N.F.

Yakima

HANFORD REACH

Snake

Pomeroy

Chehalis

Chehalis

GIFFORD

Toppenish

NAT. MON.

Lake
Sacajawea

Dayton

Clarkston

Snake

Cowlitz

PINCHOT

YAKAMA

Yakima

Pasco

McNARY N.W.R.

MT. ST. HELENS
NAT.
VOLCANIC
MON.

INDIAN

Prosser

Richland

Lake Wallula

Walla Walla

UMATILLA

Kelso

NATIONAL

RESERVATION

Kennewick

Columbia

Plateau

Blue Mountains

NATIONAL

Longview

Lewis

FOREST

CONBOY LAKE
N.W.R.

Klickitat

Goldendale

Columbia

FOREST

Vancouver

Camas

COLUMBIA RIVER GORGE
NAT. SCENIC AREA

CASCADE

IDAHO

OREGON

N

◀ Tulips are big business in the **Skagit Valley**, where thousands of these colorful flowers burst into bloom every spring.

▲ An orca swims near the **San Juan Islands**. Also known as killer whales, orcas are really a type of dolphin.

Wyoming

Land & Water
The Rocky Mountains, Yellowstone National Park, and the Green River are important land and water features of Wyoming.

Statehood
Wyoming became the 44th state in 1890.

People & Places
Wyoming's population is 532,668. Cheyenne is the state capital and the largest city.

Fun Fact
Wyoming is called the Equity State because it was the first state to give women the right to vote, granted in 1869 when it was still a territory.

▲ Steam and water from Old Faithful Geyser in **Yellowstone National Park** erupt more than 100 feet (30 m) into the air.

Map Key

★   State capital
●●●   City or town
⋯⋯   Boundary
▢   Indian Reservation
▢   National Monument
     National Park
     National Recreation Area
▢   National Forest
▢   National Grassland
▢   National Wildlife Refuge

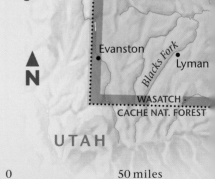

(Map of Wyoming showing: Madison, Yellowstone, Lamar, YELLOWSTONE, Yellowstone Lake, Old Faithful, NAT. PARK, Continental Divide, TARGHEE, JOHN D. ROCKEFELLER, JR. MEM. PKWY., Snake, Jackson Lake, BRIDGER, NATIONAL, GRAND TETON NATIONAL PARK, Gros Ventre, NATIONAL ELK REFUGE, FOREST, Snake, Jackson, TETON, IDAHO, Teton Range, CARIBOU, Greys, Wyoming Range, Green, NAT., Afton, NATIONAL, FOREST, Bear, Fontenelle Reservoir, FOSSIL BUTTE NAT. MON., Hams Fork, Kemmerer, Evanston, Blacks Fork, Lyman, N, WASATCH-CACHE NAT. FOREST, UTAH)

0   50 miles
0   75 kilometers

Wyoming State Flag

**Indian Paintbrush
State Flower**

**Western Meadowlark
State Bird**

◄ The Wyoming State Capitol building in **Cheyenne** was completed in 1890. It is now a U.S. national historic landmark.

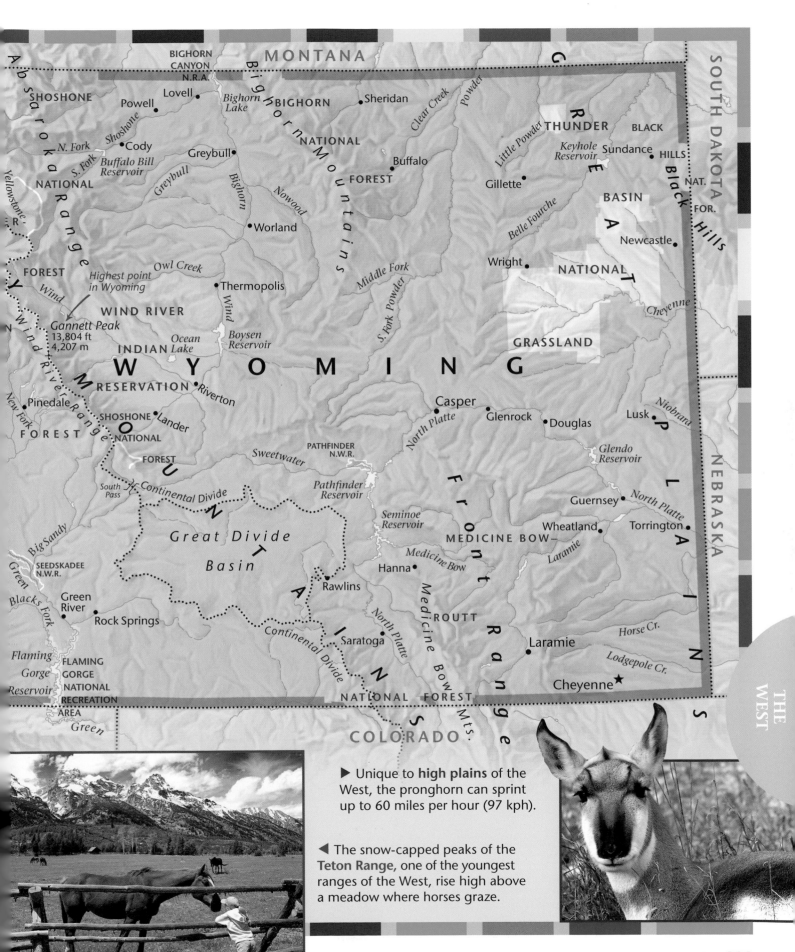

SHOSHONE

Powell · · Lovell

Bighorn Lake

BIGHORN CANYON N.R.A.

MONTANA

BIGHORN

· Sheridan

THUNDER

BLACK

SOUTH DAKOTA

Absaroka Range

N. Fork Shoshone

· Cody

Greybull ·

Shoshone

Buffalo Bill Reservoir

NATIONAL

Greybull

Bighorn

Nowood

Bighorn Mountains

NATIONAL

FOREST

· Buffalo

Clear Creek

Powder

Little Powder

Keyhole Reservoir

Sundance

HILLS

NAT.

· Gillette

Belle Fourche

BASIN

FOR.

Black Hills

Yellowstone R.

FOREST

· Worland

Owl Creek

· Thermopolis

Wright ·

NATIONAL

· Newcastle

Cheyenne

Wind

Highest point in Wyoming

WIND RIVER

Wind

GRASSLAND

Gannett Peak 13,804 ft 4,207 m

Ocean Lake

Boysen Reservoir

Wind River Range

INDIAN

W Y O M I N G

RESERVATION

· Riverton

Pinedale ·

New Fork

SHOSHONE · Lander

NATIONAL

Casper ·

Glenrock

· Douglas

Lusk ·

Niobrara

North Platte

Glendo Reservoir

PLAINS

FOREST

FOREST

PATHFINDER N.W.R.

Sweetwater

South Pass

Continental Divide

Pathfinder Reservoir

MOUNTAINS

Front Range

Guernsey ·

North Platte

Big Sandy

SEEDSKADEE N.W.R.

Great Divide Basin

Seminoe Reservoir

MEDICINE BOW

Wheatland ·

· Torrington

Laramie

Green

Blacks Fork

Green River ·

· Rock Springs

Continental Divide

Rawlins ·

Medicine Bow ·

Hanna ·

Medicine Bow

ROUTT

Laramie

Horse Cr.

NEBRASKA

Flaming Gorge Reservoir

FLAMING GORGE NATIONAL RECREATION AREA

Continental Divide

Saratoga ·

North Platte

Medicine Bow Mts.

· Laramie

Lodgepole Cr.

Green

NATIONAL FOREST

Cheyenne ★

COLORADO

THE WEST

▶ Unique to **high plains** of the West, the pronghorn can sprint up to 60 miles per hour (97 kph).

◀ The snow-capped peaks of the **Teton Range,** one of the youngest ranges of the West, rise high above a meadow where horses graze.

The Territories

The Territories
ACROSS TWO SEAS

Listed below are the five largest* of the 14 U.S. territories, along with their flags and key information. Two of these are in the Caribbean Sea, and the other three are in the Pacific Ocean. Can you find the other nine U.S. territories on the map?

U.S. CARIBBEAN TERRITORIES

PUERTO RICO
Area: 3,508 sq mi (9,086 sq km)
Population: 3,929,000
Capital: San Juan
Population 2,605,000
Languages: Spanish, English

U.S. VIRGIN ISLANDS
Area: 149 sq mi (386 sq km)
Population: 109,000
Capital: Charlotte Amalie
Population 52,000
Languages: English, Spanish or Spanish Creole, French or French Creole

U.S. PACIFIC TERRITORIES

AMERICAN SAMOA
Area: 77 sq mi (199 sq km)
Population: 67,000
Capital: Pago Pago
Population 55,000
Language: Samoan

NORTHERN MARIANA ISLANDS
Area: 184 sq mi (477 sq km)
Population: 82,000
Capital: Saipan
Population 75,000
Languages: Philippine languages, Chinese, Chamorro, English

GUAM
Area: 217 sq mi (561 sq km)
Population: 171,000
Capital: Hagåtña (Agana)
Population 144,000
Languages: English, Chamorro, Philippine languages

OTHER U.S. TERRITORIES
Baker Island, Howland Island, Jarvis Island, Johnston Atoll, Kingman Reef, Midway Islands, Navassa Island, Palmyra Atoll, Wake Island

*Close-up views of the five largest territories are highlighted in pull-out maps and labeled with a letter. You can see where each territory is located by looking for its corresponding letter on the main map.

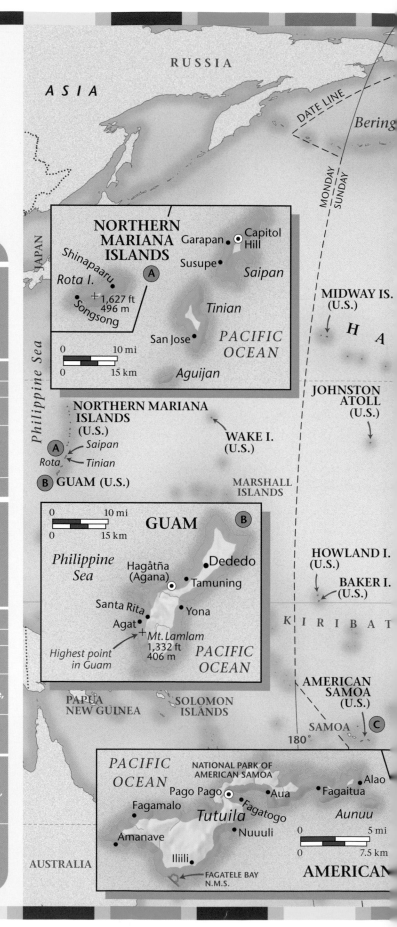

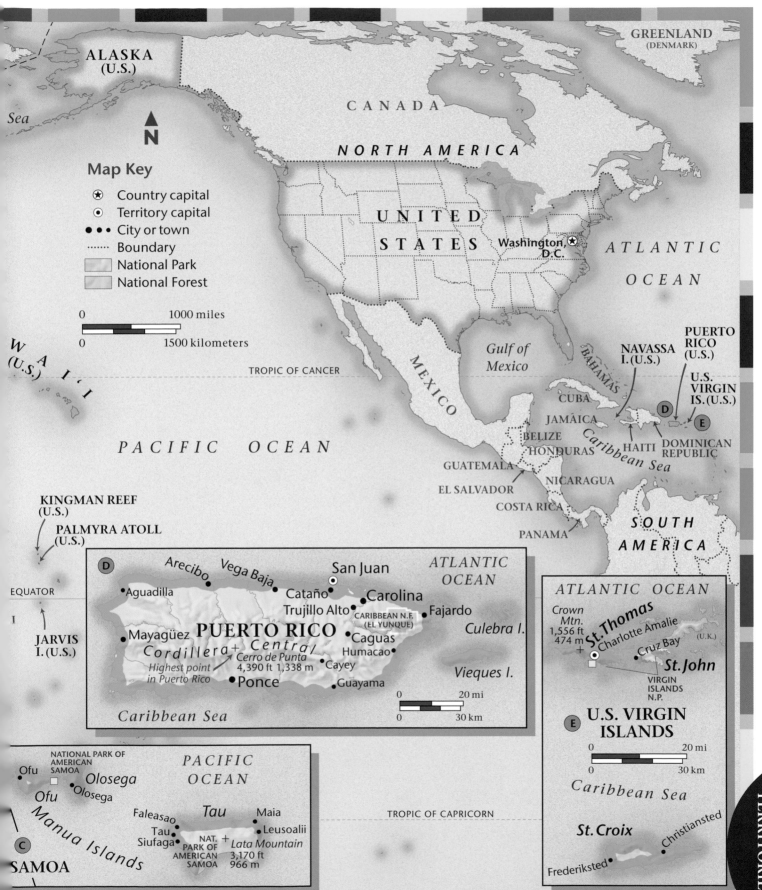

GREENLAND
(DENMARK)

ALASKA
(U.S.)

Sea

Map Key

⊛ Country capital
⊙ Territory capital
• • • City or town
. . . . . Boundary
☐ National Park
☐ National Forest

0   1000 miles
0   1500 kilometers

CANADA

NORTH AMERICA

UNITED
STATES

Washington, ⊛
D.C.

ATLANTIC

OCEAN

TROPIC OF CANCER

Gulf of
Mexico

MEXICO

PACIFIC   OCEAN

BAHAMAS

NAVASSA
I. (U.S.)

PUERTO
RICO
(U.S.)

U.S.
VIRGIN
IS. (U.S.)

Ⓓ

Ⓔ

CUBA

JAMAICA

Caribbean
Sea

HAITI

DOMINICAN
REPUBLIC

BELIZE
HONDURAS

GUATEMALA

EL SALVADOR

NICARAGUA

COSTA RICA

PANAMA

SOUTH

AMERICA

KINGMAN REEF
(U.S.)

PALMYRA ATOLL
(U.S.)

EQUATOR

I

JARVIS
I. (U.S.)

H
A
W
A
I
I
(U.S.)

Ⓓ

Arecibo   Vega Baja   San Juan   ATLANTIC
                                  OCEAN
• Aguadilla   Cataño ⊙
              Trujillo Alto   Carolina
• Mayagüez   PUERTO RICO   CARIBBEAN N.F.   Fajardo
          Cordillera + Central   (EL YUNQUE)   Culebra I.
          Highest point   Cerro de Punta   Caguas
          in Puerto Rico   4,390 ft 1,338 m   Humacao
                    Cayey
          • Ponce   Guayama   Vieques I.
                         0   20 mi
Caribbean Sea   0   30 km

ATLANTIC OCEAN

Crown   St. Thomas
Mtn.   Charlotte Amalie   (U.K.)
1,556 ft
474 m   + ⊙   • Cruz Bay
              Charlotte Amalie   St. John
                    VIRGIN
                    ISLANDS
                    N.P.
Ⓔ U.S. VIRGIN
    ISLANDS

0   20 mi
0   30 km

Caribbean Sea

St. Croix   Christiansted

Frederiksted •

NATIONAL PARK OF
AMERICAN
SAMOA

Ofu   ☐
       Olosega
Ofu   • Olosega
           Tau
Faleasao   Maia
Tau   • Leusoalii
Siufaga NAT.
         PARK OF   + Lata Mountain
         AMERICAN   3,170 ft
Ⓒ   SAMOA   966 m

PACIFIC

OCEAN

Manua Islands

SAMOA

TROPIC OF CAPRICORN

THE
TERRITORIES

The United States at a Glance

Land
Five Largest States by Area

1. **Alaska:** 663,267 sq mi (1,717,854 sq km)
2. **Texas:** 268,581 sq mi (695,621 sq km)
3. **California:** 163,696 sq mi (423,970 sq km)
4. **Montana:** 147,042 sq mi (380,838 sq km)
5. **New Mexico:** 121,590 sq mi (314,915 sq km)

Water
Primary Water Bodies Bordering the U.S.

1. **Pacific Ocean:** 65,436,200 sq mi (169,479,000 sq km)
2. **Atlantic Ocean:** 35,338,500 sq mi (91,526,400 sq km)
3. **Arctic Ocean:** 5,390,000 sq mi (13,960,100 sq km)
4. **Gulf of Mexico:** 591,430 sq mi (1,531,810 sq km)

Highest, Longest, Largest

The numbers below show locations on the map.

❶ **Highest Mountain**
Mount McKinley (Denali), in Alaska:
20,320 ft (6,194 m)

❷ **Longest River System**
Mississippi–Missouri: 3,710 mi (5,971 km)

❸ **Largest Freshwater Lake**
Lake Superior:
31,700 sq mi (82,103 sq km)

❹ **Largest Saltwater Lake**
Great Salt Lake, in Utah:
1,700 sq mi (4,403 sq km)

❺ **Northern most point**
Point Barrow, Alaska

❻ **Southern most point**
Kalae, Hawai'i

❼ **Eastern most point**
Sail Rock, West Quoddy Head, Maine

❽ **Western most point**
Peaked Island,
Attu Island, Alaska

People

More than 300 million people live in the United States, with about 53 percent of the population living in coastal regions. If the entire population of the U.S. were to stand shoulder to shoulder, everyone would fit into about 44 square miles, an area smaller than the size of Washington, D.C.

Five Largest States by Number of People

1. **California:** 36,756,666 people
2. **Texas:** 24,326,974 people
3. **New York:** 19,490,297 people
4. **Florida:** 18,328,340 people
5. **Illinois:** 12,901,563 people

Five Largest Cities* by Number of People

1. **New York City, NY:** 8,274,527 people
2. **Los Angeles, CA:** 3,834,340 people
3. **Chicago, IL:** 2,836,658 people
4. **Houston, TX:** 2,208,180 people
5. **Phoenix, AZ:** 1,552,259 people

*Figures are for city proper, not metropolitan area.

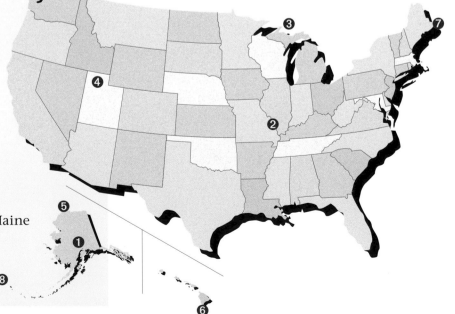

Glossary

Barrier Island: a long sandy island that runs parallel to a shore

Bicentennial: the two-hundredth anniversary of an event

Big Ten Conference: a group of colleges and universities, mostly in the Midwest, known for their sports and academic achievements

Boundary: an imaginary line that separates one political or mapped area from another; physical features, such as mountains and rivers, or latitude and longitude lines sometimes act as boundaries

Capital: a place where a country or state government is located

Coniferous forest: evergreen, needleleaf trees that bear seeds in cones

Container ships: large ships that carry goods in truck-sized metal containers among ports around the world

Continental Divide: a natural boundary line that separates the waters that flow into the Atlantic Ocean and Gulf of Mexico from the waters that flow into the Pacific Ocean

Deciduous forests: species of trees, including oak, maple, and beech, all of which lose their leaves in the cold season

Desert: a region with either hot or cold temperatures that receives 10 inches (25 cm) or less of precipitation a year

Earthquake: shaking and vibration of the earth caused by underground movement

Erosion: the process of wearing away Earth's surface by wind, water, or ice

Estuary: the wide part of a river near a sea, where freshwater and saltwater mix

Exports: products made in one place and sent to another to be sold

Foothills: a region of lower hills at the base of a mountain

Freshwater lakes: bodies of water that are surrounded by land and are not salty

Governor: the head of a state government

Grassland: large areas of mainly flat land covered with grasses

Hydroelectric plant: a facility that uses the motion of water to create power

Ice cap: an area of ice and snow that permanently covers a large area of land

Indian Reservation/I.R.: an area of land set aside by the U.S. government for Native Americans to live on and govern

Livestock: tame animals like cows and horses raised for profit

Pedestrians: people who travel on foot

Peninsula: a large piece of land that sticks out into the water

Petroleum: an energy resource that occurs naturally underground

Powwow: a council or meeting of Native Americans

Rain forest: a region occurring mostly in a belt between the Tropic of Cancer and the Tropic of Capricorn in areas that have at least 80 inches (200 cm) of rain each year and an average yearly temperature of 77°F (25°C)

Seaport: a place where seagoing ships can dock

Sedimentary: a kind of rock made of compressed small particles

Shakers: members of a religious group who did not marry and lived in communal societies

Skyline: the outline of buildings and objects in a city seen against the sky

Territory: land under the rule of a country but that is not a state or a province of that country

Thoroughbred: a breed of horse known for its speed in horse racing; a cross between Arabian stallions and English mares

Totem poles: a post with carvings and paintings that represent family histories; found especially among native peoples of the Pacific Northwest region

Tundra: a region at high latitudes or high elevations that has cold temperatures, low vegetation, and a short growing season

UFO (short for unidentified flying object): An object seen in the sky that some people believe may be flown by beings from outer space

Wetland: land that is either covered with or soaked by water; includes swamps, marshes, and bogs

Index

Pictures and the text that describes them have their page numbers printed in **bold** type.

Two-Letter Postal Codes

ALABAMA	AL
ALASKA	AK
ARIZONA	AZ
ARKANSAS	AR
CALIFORNIA	CA
COLORADO	CO
CONNECTICUT	CT
DELAWARE	DE
DISTRICT OF COLUMBIA	DC
FLORIDA	FL
GEORGIA	GA
HAWAI'I	HI
IDAHO	ID
ILLINOIS	IL
INDIANA	IN
IOWA	IA
KANSAS	KS
KENTUCKY	KY
LOUISIANA	LA
MAINE	ME
MARYLAND	MD
MASSACHUSETTS	MA
MICHIGAN	MI
MINNESOTA	MN
MISSISSIPPI	MS
MISSOURI	MO
MONTANA	MT
NEBRASKA	NE
NEVADA	NV
NEW HAMPSHIRE	NH
NEW JERSEY	NJ
NEW MEXICO	NM
NEW YORK	NY
NORTH CAROLINA	NC
NORTH DAKOTA	ND
OHIO	OH
OKLAHOMA	OK
OREGON	OR
PENNSYLVANIA	PA
PUERTO RICO	PR
RHODE ISLAND	RI
SOUTH CAROLINA	SC
SOUTH DAKOTA	SD
TENNESSEE	TN
TEXAS	TX
UTAH	UT
VERMONT	VT
VIRGINIA	VA
WASHINGTON	WA
WEST VIRGINIA	WV
WISCONSIN	WI
WYOMING	WY

Published by the National Geographic Society

John M. Fahey, Jr.
President and Chief Executive Officer

Gilbert M. Grosvenor
Chairman of the Board

Tim T. Kelly
President, Global Media Group

John Q. Griffin
President, Publishing

Nina D. Hoffman
Executive Vice President; President, Book Publishing Group

Melina Gerosa Bellows
Executive Vice President, Children's Publishing

Prepared by the Book Division

Nancy Laties Feresten
Vice President, Editor in Chief, Children's Books

Bea Jackson
Director of Design and Illustrations, Children's Books

Jennifer Emmett
Executive Editor, Reference and Solo, Children's Books

Amy Shields
Executive Editor, Series, Children's Books

Carl Mehler
Director of Maps

R. Gary Colbert
Production Director

Jennifer A. Thornton
Managing Editor

Staff for this Book

Priyanka Lamichhane
Project Editor

Bea Jackson
Art Director

Lori Renda
Illustrations Editor

Ruthie Thompson
Designer

Michael McNey, Sven M. Dolling
Map Research and Production

Martha Sharma
Writer and Chief Consultant

Erica Rose
Copy Editor

Connie Binder
Indexer

Kathryn Murphy
Editorial Intern

Grace Hill
Associate Managing Editor

Heidi Vincent
Vice President, Direct Response Sales and Marketing

Jeff Reynolds
Marketing Director, Children's Books

Lewis R. Bassford
Production Manager

Susan Borke
Legal and Business Affairs

Manufacturing and Quality Management

Christopher A. Liedel
Chief Financial Officer

Phillip L. Schlosser
Vice President

Chris Brown
Technical Director

Nicole Elliott, Rachel Faulise
Managers

Founded in 1888, the National Geographic Society is one of the largest nonprofit scientific and educational organizations in the world. It reaches more than 285 million people worldwide each month through its official journal, NATIONAL GEOGRAPHIC, and its four other magazines; the National Geographic Channel; television documentaries; radio programs; films; books; videos and DVDs; maps; and interactive media. National Geographic has funded more than 8,000 scientific research projects and supports an education program combating geographic illiteracy.

For more information, please call 1-800-NGS LINE (647-5463) or write to the following address:

NATIONAL GEOGRAPHIC SOCIETY
1145 17th Street N.W., Washington, D.C. 20036-4688 U.S.A.

Visit us online at www.nationalgeographic.com/books

ISBN 978-1-4263-0512-2 (trade); 978-1-4263-0558-0 (reinforced library binding)

Illustrations Credits

Abbreviations for terms appearing below: (t)top; (b)-bottom; (l)-left; (r)-right; (c)-center; AL = Alamy; CO = Corbis; GI = Getty Images; IS = iStockPhoto; NGS = NationalGeographicStock.com; PD = PhotoDisc; SS= Shutterstock

Art for state flowers and state birds by Robert E. Hynes

Front cover, Steve Niedorf Photography/The Image Bank/Getty Images

Back cover, (tl), Taylor S. Kennedy/NGS; (tr), italianestro/SS; (br), Glenn Taylor/IS; (bl), Michael Nichols/NGS

Front of the Book
2 (l), Alaska Stock Images/NGS; 2 (tr), SergeyIT/SS; 2 (br), metalstock/SS; 3 (tl), Zuzule/SS; 3 (tr), Eric Isselée/SS; 3 (cl), James M Phelps, Jr/SS; 3 (cr), Geoffrey Kuchera/SS; 3 (bl), 88 (l), Zuzule/SS; 6 (l), erllre74/SS; 6 (tr), Charles Krebs/Riser/GI; 6 (cr), Mike Brake/SS; 6 (br), James Randklev/Riser/GI; 7, Olivier Le Queinec/SS; 8 (t), Billy Hustace/Stone/GI; 8 (b), Sonya Etchison/SS; 9 (l), Mark R/SS; 9 (r), Pete Seaward/Stone/GI; 10 (l), PD; 10–11, PD; 11 (tr), Taylor S. Kennedy/NGS; 11 (b), Adam Woolfitt/CO

The Northeast
12 (l), Alaska Stock Images/NGS; 12–13, Skip Brown/NGS; 14 up, Shawn Pecor/SS; 14 (b), Donald Gargano/SS; 15, Joel Sartore/NGS; 16 (t), Jake Rajs/Stome/GI; 16 (c), Kevin Fleming/CO; 16 (b), William S. Kuta/AL; 17, Catherine Lane/IS; 18 (t), PD; 18 (c), Mikael Damkier/SS; 18 (b), Jeff Schultes/SS; 19, Noah Strycker/SS; 20 (t), Emory Kristof/NGS; 20 (b), Jeremy Edwards/IS; 21 (t), Justine Gecewicz/IS; 21 (b), James L. Stanfield/NGS; 22 (t), Christopher Penler/SS; 22 (b), Lijuan Guo/SS; 23 (l), Chee-Onn Leong/SS; 23 (r), Brett Atkins/SS; 24 (t), Paula Stephens/SS; 24 (c), Marcel Jancovic/SS; 24 (b), Thomas & Amelia Takacs/SS; 25, Tony Campbell/SS; 26 (t), Dave Raboin/IS; 26 (c), Steve Miller/The Star-Ledger/CO; 26 (b), Aimin Tang/IS; 27 (t), Sheldon Kralstein/IS; 27 (b), Andrew F. Kazmierski/SS; 28 (t), Cathleen Abers-Kimball/IS; 28 (b), Richard Levine/AL; 29, Glenn Taylor/IS; 30, IS; 31 (t), Jeremy Edwards/IS; 31 (r), Racheal Grazias/SS; 32 (t), Yare Marketing/SS; 32 (c), Mona Makela/SS; 32 (b), Joy Brown/SS; 33, Robert Kelsey/SS; 34 (t), Thomas M Perkins/SS; 34 (b), Glenda M. Powers/SS; 35 (t), Parker Deen/IS; 35 (b), rebvt/SS

The Southeast
36 (l), SergeyIT/SS; 36–37, Maria Stenzel/NGS; 38 (t), Darryl Vest/SS; 38 (c), Kevin Fleming/CO; 38 (b), Wayne James/SS; 39, Ronnie Howard/SS; 40 (t), Jaimie Duplass/SS; 40 (b), Bill Barksdale/CO; 41, Travel Bug/SS; 42 (t), Wayne Johnson/IS; 42 (b), Alan Freed/SS; 43 (t), Varina and Jay Patel/IS; 43 (b), Valentyn Volkov/SS; 44 (t), jackweichen_gatech/SS; 44 (c), Antonio V. Oquias/SS; 44 (b), Michael Carlucci/IS; 45, Andrew F. Kazmierski/SS; 46 (t), Leon Ritter/SS; 46 (c), Craig Wactor/SS; 46 (b), Anne Kitzman/SS; 47, Neale Cousland/SS; 48 (t), Bob Sacha/CO; 48 (c), Jim Richardson/CO; 48 (b), J. Helgason/SS; 49 (t), Stephen Helstowski/SS; 49 (r), Kathryn Bell/SS; 50 (t), Vilmos Varga/SS; 50 (c), Chad Purser/IS; 50 (b), Peter Arnold, Inc./AL; 51, Mike Flippo/SS; 52 (l), Leah-Anne Thompson/SS; 52 (r), Forrest L. Smith, III/SS; 53 (l), Rob Byron/SS; 53 (r), Brad Whitsitt/SS; 54, Rafael Ramirez Lee/SS; 55 (l), Denise Kappa/SS; 55 (b), Zach Holmes/AL; 56 (t), Envision/CO; 56 (b), Bryan Busovicki/SS; 57 (l), Wayne James/SS; 57 (r), Jennifer King/SS; 58 (t), Darren K. Fisher/SS; 58 (b), Travel Bug/SS; 59 (l), graham s. klotz/SS; 59 (r), Adam Bies/SS; 60 (t), Robert Pernell/SS; 60 (c), Ken Inness/SS; 60 (t), Mary Terriberry/SS; 61, Adam Bies/SS

The Midwest
62 (l), metalstock/SS; 62–63, Jim Richardson/NGS; 64 (t), Ralf-Finn Hestoft/CO; 64 (c), Tim Boyle/GI; 64 (t), Jenny Solomon/SS; 65, Kim Karpeles/AL; 66 (t), James Steidl/SS; 66 (b), Todd Taulman/SS; 66 (c), John J. Klaiber Jr./SS; 66 (b), Melissa Farlow/NGS; 68 (t), jokter/SS; 68 (b), Madeleine Openshaw/SS; 69 (l), Steve Schneider/IS; 69 (r), Andre Jenny/AL; 70 (t), aceshot1/SS; 70 (b), Rusty Dodson/SS; 71, Bruce Dale/NGS; 72 (t), Gary Paul Lewis/SS; 72 (c), Rachel L. Sellers/SS; 72 (b), The Final Image/SS; 73, Cornelia Schaible/IS; 74 (t), Maxim Kulko/SS; 74 (c), V. J. Matthew/SS; 74 (b), Geoffrey Kuchera/SS; 75, Karla Caspari/SS; 76 (t), Neil Phillip Mey/SS; 76 (b), Jose Gil/SS; 77 (l), Tim Pleasant/SS; 77 (r), Rusty Dodson/SS; 78 (t), Bates Littlehales/NGS; 78 (b), James L. Amos/NGS; 79 (l), Joel Sartore/NGS; 79 (b), Jim Richardson/NGS; 80 (t), Ian Martin/NGS; 80 (c), Randy Olson/NGS; 80 (b), Rusty Dodson/SS; 81, iofoto/SS; 82 (t), aceshot1/SS; 82 (c), Alex Neauville/SS; 82 (b), James M Phelps, Jr/SS; 83, Rena Schild/SS; 84 (t), Werner Bollmann/Photolibrary/GI; 84 (c), Ira Block/NGS; 84 (b), iofoto/SS; 85, Danita Delimont/AL; 86 (tl), Aga/SS; 86 (tr), Brad Thompson/SS; 86 (c), Volkman K. Wentzel/NGS; 86 (b), Alvis Upitis/AgStock Images/CO; 87, Layne Kennedy/CO

The Southwest
88 (l), Zuzule/SS; 88–89, Jack Dykinga/NGS; 90 (t), Michael Nichols/NGS; 90 (c), Zschnepf/SS; 90 (b), Chris Curtis/SS; 92 (t), italianestro/SS; 92 (c), Mariusz S. Jurgielewicz/SS; 92 (b), Ralph Lee Hopkins/NGS; 94 (t), Clint Spencer/IS; 94 (b), Phil Anthony/SS; 95 (l), Lindsay Hebberd/CO; 95 (r), MWaits/SS; 96 (t), Ben Conlan/IS; 96 (c), Mira/AL; 96 (b), Rusty Dodson/SS; 97, B. Anthony Stewart/NGS

The West
98 (l), Eric Isselée/SS; 98–99, Gordon Wiltsie/NGS; 100 (t), Benoit Rousseau/IS; 100 (b), Alysta/SS; 101, Michael Pemberton/SS; 102 (t), Stas Volik/SS; 102 (c), Bates Littlehales/NGS; 102 (b), Lindsay Noechel/SS; 103, Elke Dennis/SS; 104 (t), Larsek/SS; 104 (b), PD; 105, John Kelly/Iconica/GI; 106 (t), Jarvis Gray/SS; 106 (c), Jim Sugar/CO; 106 (b), Alex Staroseltsev/SS; 107 (t), Steve Raymer/NGS; 107 (b), Jeff Hunter/Photographer's Choice/GI; 108 (t), Bryan Brazil/SS; 108 (c), Raymond Gehman/NGS; 108 (b), David P. Smith/SS; 109, Dick Durrance II/NGS; 110 (t), Noah Clayton/The Image Bank/GI; 110 (b), Doug Lemke/SS; 111 (l), Geoffrey Kuchera/SS; 111 (r), Jerry Sharp/SS; 112 (t), Andy Z./SS; 112 (c), W. Robert Moore/NGS; 112 (b), Sam Abell/NGS; 113, Danita Delimont/AL; 114 (t), Jennifer Lynn Arnold/SS; 114 (c), Rachell Coe/SS; 114–115, Peter Kunasz/SS; 115 (r), Tischenko Irina/SS; 116 (t), Grafton Marshall Smith/CO; 116 (c), Nelson Sirlin/SS; 116 (b), PD; 118 (t), Natalia Bratslavsky/SS; 118 (b), Luis Salazar/SS; 119 (l), Oksana Perkins/SS; 119 (r), Sandy Buckley/SS; 120 (t), Videowokart/SS; 120 (b), Henryk Sadura/SS; 121 (l), Peter Kunasz/SS; 121 (r), Michael Rubin/SS

For information about special discounts for bulk purchases, please contact National Geographic Books Special Sales: ngspecsales@ngs.org

For rights or permissions inquires, please contact National Geographic Books Subsidiary Rights: ngbookrights@ngs.org

Printed in the United States
09/WOR/1

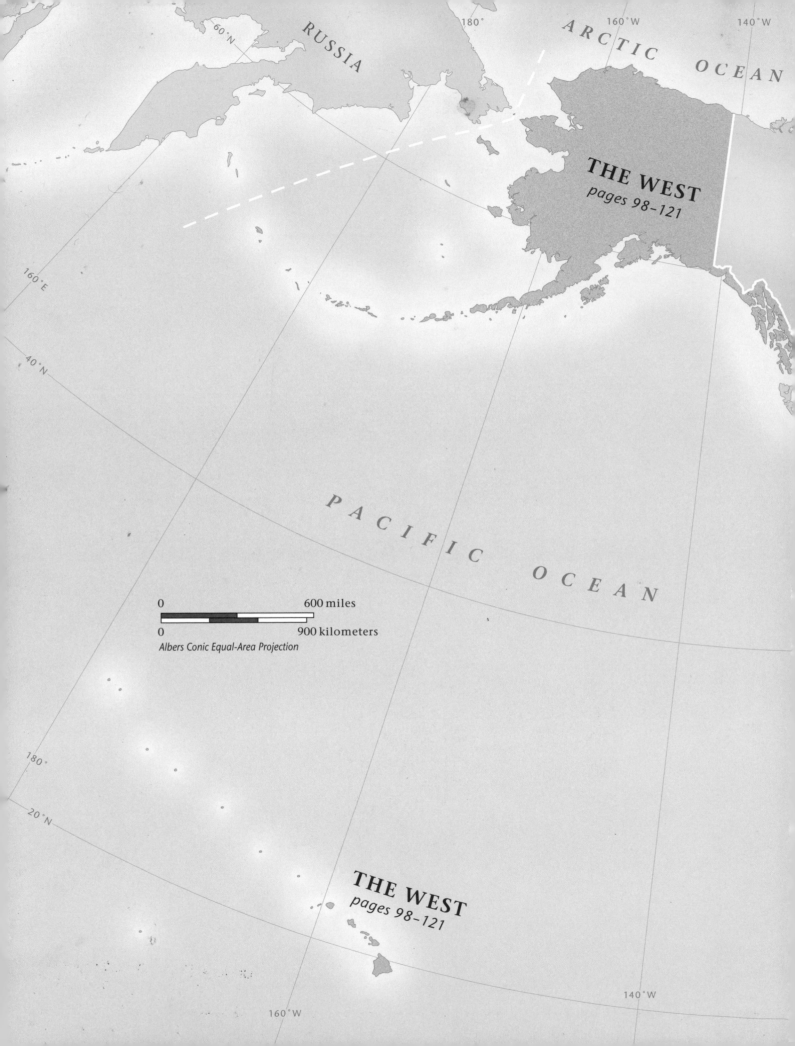

RUSSIA

ARCTIC OCEAN

THE WEST
pages 98–121

PACIFIC OCEAN

0   600 miles

0   900 kilometers

Albers Conic Equal-Area Projection

THE WEST
pages 98–121